To lee,

this is a little left... remind you how
wonderful you are on the days that you forget.
I know you're currently in a little bit of a
stormcloud but please know that you are going
to get through. you have so many people
around who absolutely adore you. They are
here to weather any storm sweetpea - to
provide umbrellas, wellies and love, always.
Please never think you are fighting alone.
you are incredible.
Heres to a brighter day.

Lots of love,

Jodi
xxx

omll xx

To Caroline, ♥

When someone treats us badly
it isn't a reflection of what we
deserve, it's a reflection of them.
The biggest, kindest hearts
get hurt the most. I hope yours
heals soon and only grows bigger
because you deserve every
happiness.   Love Jodi
                            xx

'I've known Jodi for almost seven years now. When I first met her she was an aspiring poet and like me she was just trying to get out there and play as many shows as possible. She came to watch me play at Bestival in 2011 and next thing I know, a few months later, she is paralysed. Anyone could have given up on hopes and dreams in that position, or even felt sorry for themselves. Yet every time I saw Jodi, she had regained some movement in one part of her body and slowly she was getting better.

It's a fantastic book, from a fantastic wordsmith. I'm so proud of how much Jodi has achieved since I've known her. Proper chuffed. Ed x'

Ed Sheeran

One million lovely letters.

Jodi Ann Bickley

with Kate Barker

First published in Great Britain in 2014
by Yellow Kite Books
An Imprint of Hodder & Stoughton
An Hachette UK company

1

A CIP catalogue record for this title
is available from the British Library

Chapter title image © www.shutterstock.com

Hardback ISBN 978 1 444 75478 0
eBook ISBN 978 1 444 75479 7

Typeset by Palimpsest Book Production Ltd, Falkirk, Stirlingshire
Printed and bound by CPI Group (UK) Ltd, Croydon, CR0 4YY

Hodder & Stoughton policy is to use papers that are natural,
renewable and recyclable products and made from wood grown in
sustainable forests. The logging and manufacturing processes are expected
to conform to the environmental regulations of the country of origin.

Hodder & Stoughton Ltd
338 Euston Road
London NW1 3BH

www.hodder.co.uk

Dedication

For everybody who has been involved in one million lovely letters so far - thankyou. Hopefully, I can do this forever.

xxx

Contents

vii

Foreword

I'm sitting at my desk, covered in glitter, with felt-tip pen marks up to my elbows. I hope to write ten more letters before my hospital appointment this afternoon. I've been feeling very tired this week, but I try to ignore that. There's a lot to be done.

I glance at my laptop and see that there's another email in my inbox. This one has come all the way from New Zealand! I want to read it, to find out who it's from, but stop myself. I've got to finish the task in hand.

There – one more letter done. The notepaper I'm using, a present from a lady in America, is a buttery yellow colour, so I put it in a pale blue envelope and add it to the pile ready for the postbox. I like making the envelopes beautiful too; as small pleasures go, there are not many more magical than seeing a pretty, handwritten envelope fall through the letterbox onto the mat. A little handwritten treasure: when was the last time you wrote one? It's unusual to write a letter these days, or to receive one. But it's a lovely thing to do, and it will make someone's day a little bit brighter.

If you'd told me two years ago that I would be spending a lot of my time hand-writing letters to people I had never met before, I would have laughed at you. But then two years ago my life was pretty different. These days I know that for the price of a stamp, you can change someone's day.

So why not dig that biro out of the kitchen drawer, and find the stationery set you were given a few birthdays ago? Go on – tell someone how wonderful they are. Sometimes we all need a little reminder. If you're not convinced, read on, and hopefully my story will change your mind.

Chapter one
Everything can change

Dear Jodi (aged 22),

You look amazing! Stop worrying about how big your arms are because they aren't. Stop being a div. I'm here to tell you a few things. Firstly, I'm you. It's 2013 and Twiggy and Musa are about to come over for tortillas in your brightly coloured little house. Josh is currently covered in hair dye, because he decided to jump in the shower whilst you were washing it off. You are now a red head (again!). Who is Josh? Josh is your puppy. He isn't the only new furry member of the household but I shall leave the rest as a surprise for you.

I'm not going to ruin too much for you but I do need to tell you something. Some of the most extraordinary things are going to happen to you in the next two and a half years. Remember when you first went on the Sky Rocket ride at Drayton Manor Park and they left you upside-down just a little too long? Remember that feeling? Well, life is going to cause that feeling. For a while you will

feel out of control and won't be able to do anything
about it. But from this end I can promise you that it
turns out magically. Not quite as you'd expected maybe,
but it will all work out.
Big love,
Jodi (aged 25)
xx

None of us expects that something very bad might
happen out of the blue. Something that will tip your
entire life upside-down, inside-out, and won't even leave
you a map to navigate this topsy-turvy world you thought
you had figured out. But in an instant, everything can
change – just like that.

And for me, in an instant, everything did. I contracted
a brain infection called meningoencephalitis. I know, I'd
never heard of it either.

I was 23 and had been performing at a music festival
on the Isle of Wight. I'd gone with Sarah, one of my best
friends. We had an amazing time and returned with
pockets full of glitter, empty hip flasks and a bunch of
memories sound tracked by our favourite bands. I started
feeling a bit poorly a week after I came home – nothing
you could put your finger on, just not quite right. I put
it down to tiredness and having overdone it during the
summer.

When I woke up on 27 September 2011, about two

weeks after I got home to Birmingham, I had what felt like the worst-ever case of flu. I rang my mum to ask when she was coming home and she told me to phone the GP. But my GP is never available. Someone came up with the amazing idea that every doctors' surgery in our area should be merged into one super-duper doctors' surgery, but now you have to book an appointment two weeks before you even feel ill. Instead I made an appoint-ment at a walk-in centre and my brother Jake drove me there. I remember sitting on the floor in the waiting room, looking at all the other people in the queue and asking the receptionist if it was my turn yet. I'm not usually like that; usually I would sit quietly until they closed before I uttered a word, but that day I couldn't handle people talking and felt completely disorientated. Perhaps I had a high temperature. Suddenly I had to leave. I cancelled the appointment and my brother took me home again.

Normally Jake teases me for being pale because he is blessed with olive skin whereas I am practically transparent on a good day and look like death warmed up when I'm poorly. But he didn't tease this time. He asked if I was all right and then just drove. Mum was home when I got back. Thankfully, she could see I wasn't just a bit under the weather, that this wasn't simply a bad cold, and she took me to the walk-in clinic opposite the hospital. She later told me that I had gone a horrible grey colour, my eyes were sunken and my lips were turning blue.

The GP at the walk-in clinic got me to lie on the bed while he examined me from head to toe. I felt terrible by this point but I was still with it enough to see that he and Mum were worried. I explained that I had flu-like symptoms, only much worse than I'd ever experienced with flu before. Then the GP found a mark on my foot, a little circular red insect bite with bruising around it. He asked where I had been recently, and if I had been bitten by any insects. Mum told him that I'd been at a festival on the Isle of Wight, and I remembered I'd been bitten loads of times there. The GP then said he thought I had contracted meningoencephalitis from a tick bite. He wanted to phone for an ambulance to take me to the hospital over the road, but there wasn't time. By this point everything was going pretty blurry and walking was becoming a challenge. Mum and the GP bundled me into a wheelchair and rushed me straight to the hospital Accident and Emergency department. Within 20 minutes I was unconscious.

I have no memory of anything that happened over the next two days. I'm told I was immediately given two different types of medicine via a drip going into my arm. The doctors gave me a lumbar puncture – otherwise known as a spinal tap – in which a needle is stuck into your spine. They needed to test the spinal fluid to check for signs of infection and they also had to drain some off because there was so much pressure on my spinal column.

Then I had a scan to see what was going on in my brain. Mum says that I kept saying 'thank you' to everyone, but I don't remember.

Mum gets very wobbly whenever she talks about that time, which isn't often if she can help it. She says it was a complete nightmare as encephalitis is life-threatening. For a couple of days no-one knew which way it was going to go.

What happened to me was unusual, but it can happen to anyone. Around one person in 200,000 gets encephalitis if they are bitten by a tick. Just one little pesky tick bite, and you can die from it. But I didn't die. Instead, that one moment changed my life in ways I could never possibly have imagined.

Chapter two
The letter made things OK.

23 March 1993

To Nanny
c/o God
The Sky
Heaven
H34 V3N

Dear Nanny,
I hope you are having fun in Heaven. Mummy told me it
is good up there. I hope you can watch me go to the
Teddy Bears' Picnic this week. You are the best Nanny
in the whole world. I miss you and love you all around
the world and back again.
Lots of love,
Jodi
X

grew up in Tyseley, Birmingham, a place my mum always referred to as Hall Green because it sounds nicer. In Tyseley, lads inherit their fathers' reputations and girls make theirs depending on how long it takes them to do it behind the monkey bars in the park none of us were supposed to go into but did. Tyseley used to be full of factories, with loads of jobs for local people, but it has been on the slide for a long time. There haven't been enough jobs here for many years. Now the women stay at home and the men work in local garages, construction or narcotics. You have to be a bit careful if you're out round here at night, especially if you're a lad.

There may not be much money in Tyseley but there are a lot of very kind people who help out when they can. At the top of the road you will still find Deeta's corner shop, which has been there for as long as anyone can remember but looks more and more dated every year. Deeta has a generous heart and if you don't have enough money, sometimes he lets you have things on tick. Across the road from Deeta's is Meeka's off-licence. Meeka is a true eccentric who sets the price of his goods depending on how he's feeling that day. Most of the time he's pretty reasonable.

At the bottom of our road there's a chocolate factory. Well, it used to be a chocolate factory. Sounds great, doesn't it? I remember the smell from when I was younger, a smell of melting chocolate that I knew I should like but didn't. It made me feel a bit sick. These days the old factory is mainly used as a warehouse for providing tat to shops with names like 'Bargain Binz'. I distinctly remember it being a clothes shop and a cake shop but no-one else does so I may have made this up.

Anyway, on a wide, mostly sleepy street amongst a bunch of terraced ex-council houses you will find the house we moved to when I was five, where my family still lives. I've catapulted back there a few times since I've been a so-called grown-up, and I'll probably do it again some day. My mum has always had huge decorating dreams but we've never had the money. She lusts after the transformations on *60 Minute Makeover* and *DIY SOS*. I often wish I could fit the whole of B&Q and all those quirky independent shops into my pockets and do up the house for her.

As soon as you walk in you step onto a square metre of red tiles with coats hanging up to the right, which we call our entrance hall. The smell hits you straight away – chain smoking masked by vanilla-scented candles and Nescafé coffee. In front of you are stairs up to the bedrooms and to the left are the living room and kitchen. If you look up at the ceiling you'll see one of my mum's most prized possessions, a light fixture that once belonged to my grandparents. It's made from lots of pieces of stained glass and glows red, yellow, blue and green when the bulb is on. It has no value to anyone outside the family but just knowing it's there has always filled me with a sense of security. As children my brother and I liked to stand beneath the light in the hall, turning the switch on and off to make the stained glass flicker like a Christmas tree.

Our living room, kitchen and bathroom all connect. I've been in houses where the living room is as big as the entire ground floor of my mum's house and I just wouldn't know how to make that kind of space feel homely. I guess it's different strokes for different folks but I feel happiest in organised chaos. Everything at Mum's is piled on top of something – clothes, dogs, children. Getting anywhere is like navigating an obstacle course and if you sit down for even a second you will find a large loveable lump of a dog is trying to climb onto your lap. The house would definitely not feature in *Ideal Home* magazine but it felt like home to me.

Mum is a hoarder and I've inherited the instinct. I've still got boxes and boxes full of memories: letters and notes and old school books; scraps of paper with boys' names and mine interlinked and loads of love hearts drawn in neon colours. Aged eleven I promised myself that I'd keep everything that ever meant something, and I have. I'm going to end up being on that TV show *Hoarders* where people have to chuck out all the clutter they don't need any more. But I think memories and mementos are important. I still have a note passed by a guy in my college class. It had a cartoon drawing of me and underneath it said 'My name is Jodi and I have pretty eyes'. Anyone else would wonder why I had kept that, but it mattered to me and things that matter are kept.

There are three bedrooms at Mum's. Actually, more like two and a half. One is really a box room and that was mine. If ever I felt stressed about anything I would move my furniture around, as if I would one day discover the secret solution to making more space. But of course there was no solution to be found; it was a box room and there was no more space. My brother Jake's room was longer and narrow. We swapped when we were younger, then swapped back. I guess I roped him into my space-finding schemes.

My mum's bedroom is chaotic, much like the rest of the house. I don't think she has ever thrown away an item of clothing, and she'll definitely be OK for clothes if rationing ever comes back. Hers is the biggest of the three bedrooms. I've never understood why some children have bigger rooms than their parents. I always thought it was a given that the biggest room comes with the greatest responsibility. Besides, there are two parents to fit into one room.

Well, sometimes there are two parents. With me, mostly there weren't. For a long time, my mum brought my brother and me up on her own.

My mum is five foot six inches tall – but swears she is

taller – with a mass of brown hair on her head and freckles covering her face. She is my best friend in the world. The last and only argument we had was when I was eleven and Joanne down the road taught me how to wiggle my bum. Mum didn't like this at all. I soon realised she was right, as always, and my bum remained unwiggled until many years later when I got into 90s R&B and couldn't stop myself.

Mum doesn't have a laugh but an infectious cackle and she rarely stops talking, even if it's only to her dogs. At 53 she still hasn't quite mastered the art of having an 'inside voice'. I've become more aware of this as I've got older. It doesn't matter where we are – she has one volume and channel, which is loud and very Brummie. She talks as if she is using the device we kids used to talk to each other from different rooms – two paper cups linked by a long piece of string. My Mum has a heart Florence Nightingale would have approved of. She is just really, really good. She has time for everyone and always helps out when help is needed, popping round to check on neighbours if they're not well, and often giving the old lady round the corner a lift to see her friend. She makes time for people, and that's how we were brought up too.

My biological father, Tony, has always been a bit useless – as he himself admits. He still hasn't worked out how to be a father and I've never called him 'dad' as a result. Tony chose not to be a part of my life, so many times.

My parents were together on and off until I was three, then my brother Jake was born and Tony all but disappeared. He would occasionally come for a visit, usually with a new girlfriend whom Mum would have to put up with for our sake. We'd play families for a while then before long he'd be off and we would be left waiting for the next visit. If we wanted to get in touch with him we would have to telephone the pub where he drank. He'd usually be there. We'd ask him to visit and he'd say sure, he'd be right over. Jake and I would stand under the stained-glass light in our entrance hall, coats on, ready to go out, until too much time had passed and it slowly dawned on us that he wasn't going to turn up. The letdown always hurt.

Tony constantly messed up. When he came back he was like a tornado, turning everything upside down and then disappearing as quickly as he had arrived, leaving my mum with the debris. She put us back together, again and again.

Tony looks like a washed-up rock and roll star, and has the attitude to match. He blames the rest of the world for the way his life has turned out. I guess it's easier to do that sometimes. He is an alcoholic and always dabbling in some sort of drug. He will say it is to escape, but I think it's to mask the guilt and shame of knowing he could have done things differently but chose not to. My brother and I have met him a few times as adults, almost always in a pub. His ideas about parenting were learned from the edge of the bar. Once he spiked my brother's lemonade with an acid tab to 'liven him up a bit'. It wasn't until later, when my brother was being comforted by my mum, who thought he was seriously ill, that we found out that it was actually just a horrendous trip and my brother's first time on drugs, aged nineteen. Mum says Tony wasn't always like that; it was the drink and drugs that made him such a let-down. But I always wonder what he had in him that the drink brought out; what was broken in him and never fixed.

Every time I see Tony I want to find he has turned it all around and made some changes. Maybe because I want to feel as if I'm worth it, that my brother and I are worth fighting for. But it never happens, and I have to accept that it probably never will. Occasionally we pass each other in the street and look the other way, pretending we haven't noticed each other. I would love to have had a caring dad but I've come to terms with the fact that I didn't. Sometimes you just have to let people go their own way and accept that their problems aren't your responsibility or your fault. I've learned the hard way that if someone really doesn't want to change then there is nothing you can do. You just have to look after yourself and be there if you're needed.

Tony wasn't there for us, so we looked elsewhere for father figures. TV was a good source of inspiration and

I thought Bill Cosby, the American wrestler 'Macho Man' Randy Savage, and Trevor McDonald would all be pretty good. The trouble was, they weren't flesh and blood. There were decent men in the neighbourhood and when I was small I used to keep a hopeful eye out for good candidates. I'm told that I asked the milkman to be my dad one morning because he seemed like a nice man. Apparently this is not how it works, I was informed, but luckily the milkman was nice enough to make a joke of it. Later, Mum suggested that we'd go and get a dad from Woolworths in the Buy One Get One Free section – and pay a visit to the pick-n-mix while we were there.

Mum loved music and my childhood was played out to a Motown and Soul soundtrack. Her parents – my nanny and granddad – loved reggae and Motown, and Mum tells stories about them slow dancing in their living room on a Sunday lunchtime to the *Billy Cotton Band Show* on the radio. I can associate every heartbreak in my life with a song, my first being my dad, of course. I vividly remember Mum and me in our tiny kitchen, clutching wooden spoons as microphones, singing 'I will always love you' by Whitney Houston at the top of our voices after another let-down, both of us a little bit broken for our own reasons. My brother Jake, then still a baby, was our audience.

I really remember from my childhood the sense that words were powerful things. That something as simple as a pop song lyric could brighten up your day, make a bad time feel bearable. That no matter what you were feeling, someone, somewhere on the planet had felt the same way too, and if you looked carefully you would probably find a genius musician who had brilliantly summed up your feelings for you.

Mum taught me to read when I was just three. The way she did it was she told us we were going to play leapfrog. She wrote down the names of our family and some friends – Mum, Jodi, Jake and so on – on little pieces of paper, then put them down on our living room floor. She would call out the names – 'Jake', 'Jodi' – and I would jump onto the word that matched what she said. Mum has never been a career woman and wasn't well-educated herself, but she has a way with words and values them. She taught me the joy of language, that words were important, and for that I can't thank her enough.

If my dad was bittersweet memories, my grandparents taught me what love looks like. They could fit a lifetime of it into a glance, a laugh or an embrace. My nanny was so beautiful. When she was seventeen, with an eighteen-inch waist, Nanny was on a beach in Weston with her friends when she was approached by *Vogue* to model. The people from *Vogue* took some photos then came all the way to her house in Birmingham to ask her to do more. Her dad was having none of it, telling her it was prostitutes' work, so she turned them down.

Months later my grandmother met my grandfather after they started to mix in the same circles. They fell passionately in love, which scared them both as they were still young, so they made a plan to separate for six months. If it was meant to last, they agreed they would meet six months later, on the corner of the street where they first met, and then they would spend their lives together. Thankfully for me, six months later they were still hopelessly in love, so they got married. My granddad smiled with his eyes, the sort of smile you can't fake because it comes from somewhere magic. Even when they were older, my granddad still lit up whenever Nanny came into a room. They were truly happy.

My grandparents were so important to me. They say it takes a village to raise a child; well, a village would help but my nanny was best. When Mum was in the hospital having my brother, my nan stayed at home with me. I got to sleep in my mum's big bed with my nan. At the time I was only three so this made me feel like a proper grown-up. I woke up in the night, distraught, thinking my nanny's head had fallen off as I pulled back the covers and was greeted by her feet. I didn't know you could even sleep that way around in bed. Nanny laughed and laughed and we both went to sleep again, the wrong way round. She showed me that anything was possible.

I can't really remember my nanny being poorly. My only memory of her being a little fragile was after an operation, when I wasn't allowed to wriggle about on her lap while she read me a story. She sent me a letter, my first-ever letter, when she was too ill to come and see us. I still have it and cherish it to this day. It's like a golden ticket to a time I've lost but hope to find again one day. Written in my nanny's flowing handwriting, which makes me think of fairytales and old films, it says:

Dearest Jodi,

I hear you have been such a good girl for Mummy and have done all that she has asked! You are such a special little girl. I'm so sorry we can't see you this week, I will wait until my cold has gone so I don't make Jake poorly. Granddad and I love you so very much, all the way around the world and back again.

Lots of love

Nanny and Granddad

Xxx

Except that Nanny didn't have a cold. She was too ill to come over because she had cancer and was having chemotherapy to treat it. My nanny fought cancer for fifteen years and swore it wouldn't be the thing that killed her. It wasn't. She died at 57, in my granddad's arms on the bathroom floor, from a blood clot passing through her heart.

I remember exactly how it sounded the moment we

heard Nanny had died. The telephone rang, my mum answered it and she let out a scream that I can only guess is the sound a heart makes when it falls to pieces. I was quickly ushered out by our neighbours, with some sweets my nanny and granddad had got me the day before. Aged four at the time, I can't say I had any idea of the enormity of what had happened. I just knew that my mum was crying and there was nothing I could do to make that stop.

Apparently the next day I skipped to school telling people that my nanny had died. My only other experience of death before this was when I was very little and was at the funeral of a family friend. I'd had birthdays so in my world candles meant celebration, and when I saw candles there, in front of the whole funeral I sang 'Happy do, happy do, happy do'. Thankfully, the whole church cracked up. I'm told the deceased would have loved it and Mum has been telling the story ever since. When Nanny died I was a little older. I knew what had happened, but didn't understand that I was never going to see her again.

A few months later I woke my mum, sobbing that I wanted my nanny. This is when my mum explained. She told me that I wasn't going to be able to see Nanny again, but that every child was allowed to write one letter to Heaven. The postman makes a special trip there but you can only write once.

So the next morning, with Mum's help, I wrote my first Lovely Letter, the one at the beginning of this chapter on page 13. Then we put a stamp on the letter and took it to the postbox. It still wasn't the same without Nanny, but the letter made things OK. And it brought my mum a bit of happiness at a tough time as well. Though I was only small, I could tell that Mum liked seeing my love for Nanny, and that made me feel good inside.

When Nanny died we moved closer to Granddad, and Tyseley, the area we moved into, was quite deprived. I changed primary schools and the new school was very different from my previous school. Mum always says that even though we didn't have much money we were always well-presented. I didn't fit in. The head teacher of the new school told Mum that I spoke too nicely, I was too polite, too pretty, and that was why I was bullied. It went on for two years. When I was seven, the bullies dragged me around the playground by my hair, the rough ground taking a huge chunk out of my hip. I was stabbed with pencils, pushed into coat pegs and kicked repeatedly. Eventually it got so bad that I began to hate going to school. I worked out that if I threw up I wouldn't have to go so I made myself sick, just the once. This made Mum realise that she had to take action, quickly, so she moved me to another school. I only made myself sick that one time, but a seed had been planted.

During the summer, Mum entertained all the kids on

our street. We didn't have any money but with her imag-
ination we didn't need any. We had a slide in our back
garden that Mum would turn into our very own Alton
Towers, with builders' plastic sheeting from the construction site and a liberal use of the hosepipe. All the kids
were invited. Even though our house was small it was
always full of people. Mum taught us all to bake, to make
greeting cards and she took us to every free activity
Birmingham had to offer. Her shoulders were cushions
for kids whose lives so far hadn't been idyllic and she
always kept her heart open no matter how many times
it had been hurt. She taught us how to be kind. It was
quite usual for Mum to have half the kids in the neighbourhood over for Sunday lunch, all sitting on the floor in
our tiny living room with plates on their laps. Children
loved being with my mum so much that at weekends she
had to put a note on the front door saying 'Don't knock
until 8.30am'. Mum is tough, but the kindest, fairest
woman in the world.

Looking back, I think my mum poured all her love and
heartbreak over her own mum's tragically early death into
trying to make other people better. Fixing other people's
hurts to fix her own. Caring for other people brought her
comfort, gave her a purpose.

That's what Mum taught me, above all else – to behave
in a loving, caring way. I think my dad is frightened by
the world, and he buries that fear in drink and drugs.

Goodness knows, Mum has enough to be frightened of as well. She's been through a lot. But the difference is Mum doesn't lash out; she's never spiteful or unkind. She doesn't act out of fear but out of love, and by being a loving person she heals herself too.

I grew even closer to Granddad after Nanny died. He was Jake's and my star player, a gorgeous man. He stayed close to us all, helping out, just being there. He thought about us all the time and showed he cared in so many lovely little ways, like buying walkie-talkies so Jake and I could have secret conversations from under the pillows when we were supposed to be asleep. When I was small I loved the band Take That, and Granddad learned all about Take That so he could talk to me about them. I was his princess and he was on our side. At one point I really, really wanted a hoodie, so he went to the market to get me one. He got it all wrong, of course, as parents and grandparents always do. The hoodie was enormous – it must have been a grown man's size. It said 'USA' on the front which was not what I wanted, and it didn't have a zip when it really needed to have a zip. But I have kept it to this day and still wear it if I'm feeling poorly.

Ian turned up when I was eight. Although I've never called him dad, he was the closest thing I had to one. Ian comes from a line of Romany Gypsies and is often covered in oil, paint or both. Gold rings cover his fingers and his wrists are scattered with tiny home-drawn tattoos that he and his friends thought were a good idea once, so you can tell his life story by looking at his hands. Ian has the broadest Birmingham accent and calls pretty much every woman he knows 'bab'. ('Bab' is part of many a Brummie's vocabulary. It falls between the words 'love' and 'babe'; 'bab', to a Brummie, is used as a term of endearment, or in Ian's case also as a swift go-to when he can't quite remember your name.) Ian had lots of old-fashioned rules that took a while to get used to, like not wearing your hat in the house, or not taking drink or food upstairs. Mum hadn't had a boyfriend since my dad and didn't want to introduce us to somebody who wasn't going to be a permanent fixture so in the early days Ian would phone the house as a character out of one of our favourite films – Mrs Doubtfire. Ian does a brilliant impression of her and had me and my brother completely convinced. Even now, when I ask him about it, he acts as though he has no idea what I mean.

When Ian moved in, a year or so later, we also inherited some brothers and a sister who came to stay at weekends. Danny was seven, Hannah was six, Ian was four and Kyle had just been born. Although Danny and Hannah were not Ian's biological children he had brought them up since they were tiny and soon they became our family too. Our ages read 8, 7, 6, 5, 4, 0 and our birthdays July 2nd, 22nd, 23rd, 24th, 30th and August 5th. Which is a funny coincidence, and also an insight into the time of year our mothers were feeling frisky. I have been scared of October ever since.

Anyone who has been a child in a stepfamily will know that it doesn't come without issues. There are lots. Before Ian came along Jake and I didn't have a dad, but we had Mum all to ourselves. She was special and she was ours. There were the three of us, and Granddad round the corner, and that was good. There wasn't much money, even though Mum worked hard looking after old ladies, but we had enough. Jake and I never went without; we always had Christmas presents and the right school uniform and despite some tough times life was pretty good.

Everything got stretched out when Ian came along. Mum was still the breadwinner and ran the household too, but suddenly there were more mouths to feed on the same money, and there wasn't quite enough to go round. Putting two different sets of kids together and expecting them not just to like each other, but also to feel love for each other, was always going to be tricky. We had the usual battles: 'You can't tell me off, you're not my mum', and so on. But the big battle was the one for Mum's attention. Before, Jake and I had had her all to ourselves. Now we had to share her with five other people too.

We slowly learned to rub along together. It was the only option. Our house was small, but the walls expanded to fit the needs of everyone inside: Ian and Mum and the baby in Mum's room, at weekends the three boys in Jake's and Hannah and me in mine. I loved singing and dancing and a lot of hard work went into the routines that I regularly made my brothers and sister perform. As the oldest I became the lead singer of our tribute version of S Club 7, which we had to stop eventually when, heartbreakingly, the band split up. Hannah and I performed as a duo for a while but we split up due to artistic differences.

Even though Mum had a new, expanded family to look after, she still found time for neighbours and friends who needed her. Our home was a halfway house for friends. We had attempted suicides and runaways to stay with us and sent them home again with everything changed for the better, as if they were newborn. My siblings and I learned about heartbreak and mistakes made while we were hidden away on the staircase, listening to the grown-ups. There were cups of tea to fix slit wrists and laughter to sellotape heartaches. My mum is an amazing tailor. She stitched all sorts back together.

One night a family friend – let's call him John – tried to take his own life. He had slit both wrists and came to my mum's because he instantly regretted what he'd done. Mum wrapped his wrists in towels and applied pressure whilst I made him laugh at the complexities of being a fourteen-year-old until the ambulance arrived. It didn't seem a big deal at the time, and it still doesn't, yet when I talk about incidents like that many people look shocked and ask how I dealt with it. It doesn't feel like something we had to 'deal' with. It's the way we were brought up. If someone needs help, you help, to the best of your ability. I knew that John would die if he didn't get help, but I also knew that the ambulance was coming and that he was in the right place to get help. Disaster had been averted. And I was proud of the fact that my mum and Ian were well thought of in the community; that John thought they would be the best people to turn to in a crisis, the safest hands to deal with a situation he regretted getting himself into.

❧

Maybe as a result of growing up with so many people around, I was a very open child. I always looked at people in the street, and I noticed when someone smiled at a stranger, or opened the door for someone else. When I was about seven and out shopping with Mum I spotted a man with a golden smile. Yes, actually golden – his whole mouth was full of gold teeth. Mum told me to stop staring but as we got closer I blurted out 'Your mouth is made of sunshine.' He smiled and said 'So is yours!' Only now I'm older do I recall his face and realise that a natural reaction would have been to be scared of him, but I've never limited my compliments to a certain type of person. Lovely encounters happened a lot. I was forever talking to strangers in supermarkets, chatting to the checkout ladies while Mum packed the shopping. I noticed small acts of kindness and appreciated them and so, on the whole, people were kind to me. Something as insignificant as moving up on a bus for an old lady might end up in a conversation. You never know what a little bit of kindness can lead to.

When I was ten I discovered a passion for poetry. We had been studying poetry in class and our teacher, Mr Brown, who was tall and gangly with a manic look in his eye, set us some homework to write a poem about the changing seasons. I went home and filled my exercise book with poems. And the next day. And the day after that. I decided that I wanted to be a journalist or an author, like J.K. Rowling, because I loved writing and knew that those jobs meant you could write all the time. My exercise book filled up with gold stars and soon I was sent to the head teacher to be congratulated on my poems. Possibly also to stop me clearing the school out of exercise books.

Being sent to the head teacher was really scary, even if it was for doing something good. To my mind, she looked like a witch – very thin, with sharp features – and everyone was terrified of her. One day my class teacher sent me to her office on an errand. I knew that the head teacher had recently been bereaved, and I knew what that meant because I had lost my nanny. I was very scared of her, but I could also tell that she was upset so I decided to hug her – and she stopped crying. She didn't eat me and that's how I knew I had done a good thing. At the age of ten, my head teacher was basically the scariest, most powerful person on the planet and for that second I had made her feel OK. She was smiling and talking to me about my poems and for that small window of time we were the same – both grateful for the other. I was grateful she hadn't bitten my head off and glad I made a little difference, even if it was just for a moment.

After that I was the head teacher's favourite. The end-of-school cup was usually given to an academic high achiever, someone who was going on to one of the grammar schools in the area. We'd speculated about it and decided a girl called Neelam would get it because she had got into an amazing school. We all sat waiting in our Oliver Twist costumes, ready for the end-of-year performance – fake dirt all over our faces, the girls in long flowing skirts as Nancy's girls and the boys in flat caps and waistcoats as Oliver's friends. The head teacher made a speech and we all turned to Neelam ready to congratulate her. But this year's speech came with a shock – the cup was being given to somebody who hadn't been at the school for the whole seven years. Everyone looked over at me and then the head teacher said my name and announced I was getting the cup for being a kind person. I wasn't the cleverest, the prettiest, the wealthiest or the most fortunate, but I learned you could achieve in other ways. Being kind had always been my mum's badge of honour, and now it was mine too.

Dear Ms Penman,

It was actually really comforting to see you upset that day. Not because it was nice to see you upset; it was just nice to see that you were real. You were human, just like me. I had built you up in my head as some sort of all-knowing, powerful ogre but with one interaction you changed all that and I'm eternally grateful. After being bullied, I'd learnt to be scared of people. I'd learnt to be fearful and came to this new school fearing everything and everyone, including you. That day when I made you feel better, you made me feel better too. I wasn't scared of you any more and you broke down a wall I had built up for the bullies. You let me know that actually it was OK to be kind and I wasn't going to get pushed into the coat pegs for it.

From then on you always told me I'd make a difference in this world, although my world at the time was made up of Spice Girls tribute bands in the playground and working out how to use the new computers. You helped restore my faith in my character and for that I am so thankful.

I hope you are enjoying retirement.

Jodi

X

Chapter three
When something makes you happy, hold onto it.

10 August 2003

MUM!
I've gone to town with Aliss, will be back at six!
I've left your mug on the side, coffee - milk - two and
a bit sugars.
All you've got to do is boil the kettle.
Yes, I used the square spoon. (Promise.)
Love you so much Mum, all the way around the world
and back again.
Jodi xxxxxxxx

I've never understood my mum's logic surrounding the square spoon. She is convinced that her coffee will only taste right if this particular spoon is used. Now, don't let the term 'square spoon' fool you. It is a regular spoon, a teaspoon with a square end. That is all – but my mum swears by its magical coffee-making powers. On rare occasions I have used a different spoon to try to catch her out and she hasn't noticed, but if I ever mention that the spoon wasn't used she'll say she had already worked it out, she just didn't want to hurt my feelings.

I always had a certain amount of freedom growing up. There was no other option for Mum but to trust me to be responsible. She worked shifts, leaving the house by 7.30am to go and look after the folk at the old people's home, and coming back about lunchtime, so we often wouldn't see each other until I got in from school. At weekends, Ian would be in the house, so there was an adult around if something went wrong, but once I was old enough I took on the role of looking after the younger ones. It was never something that was expected of me, but I really liked it. When I was old enough to go out by myself the next oldest child took the reins to boss around the younger ones.

As long as I was honest with Mum about where I was going, what I was doing and what time I was coming back, she put a lot of trust in me. Many of my friends' parents didn't have a clue what they were up to, which I guess made rebellion that bit more exciting. I never felt the need to go through those teenage rebellions of smoking and drinking. I didn't even swear until I was thirteen, which was pretty good going. I did end up going out drinking at seventeen but my mum knew about it. She knew where I was, what I was doing and she picked my friends and me up at the end of the night – then laughed at our hangovers the next day. On the couple of weekends when I overdid it, Mum came down on me like a ton of bricks. The honesty and trust we have with each other has never felt like a burden, and I can't recall a time when I wished she didn't know about something I had done. She was honest with me and told me about her own mistakes – episodes when she had done the same as me and what she had learned from the experience. This helped me learn without feeling judged. Mum always had a very strong sense of right and wrong, but was very tolerant and broad-minded with it, so I never felt I had let her down. I am immensely lucky to have this relationship.

I had a lovely time at secondary school: I got along with everyone; I always had friends who I liked to make laugh; I looked like your average teenager although nothing stood out about my appearance; my grades were good and I was never in any trouble. I was even a prefect. I was good at most subjects, except for maths. Maths and I fell out, often.

After my first burst of enthusiasm for poetry, I didn't really delve into it during my secondary school years. School poetry anthologies can have a way of draining all the joy from rhythm and rhyme. But music – lyrics as well as songs – remained very important to me. I was very in touch with the idea of love, busy working out what it meant, convincing myself I was falling in and out of it daily.

As in most schools, we would borrow a textbook for a

year then hand it back for it to be passed on to the year below. There were always messages in the back of our battered old textbooks written by previous owners: 'YOU SUCK', 'EAT SHIT', 'RICH IS FIT 4EVA' were some typical less-than-charming comments. I always wanted to find a lovely message but never did, so I wrote one in my textbook that said 'You are so pretty!' I shared this particular textbook with my friend, and in the next lesson I found 'Thank you' written under my note. I started to experiment by leaving scraps of paper with kind messages in library books, hoping they would be found by people who needed them. I kept it quiet, though. With everyone always knowing everyone else's business at school, it was nice to have a secret. I liked the idea of anonymous acts of kindness. It was as if I was in a secret club where I could write anonymous things to people – always good things – and they wouldn't know to thank me. I remembered what it was like to be bullied, and wanted to do something to cheer up anyone who was having a bad time.

I was in a happy year group. We were lucky because the experiences a lot of kids have at school aren't the greatest, but ours were. We were always laughing, falling passionately in and out of love from one day to the next. For someone whose first kiss was under a bridge, aged fourteen, with a big goth boy called Courtney who I dated for a whole day, I dished out relationship advice as if I was about to celebrate my diamond wedding anniversary.

Love was based on looks across a classroom and notes passed and conversations on MSN until midnight on a school night. Everything meant something, and it was all so exciting and new. This sense of optimism and excitement about life is something I've tried hard to hang on to, and my sensitivity, impulsiveness and open heart are products of it.

I loved passing and leaving notes around in school. I'd put little pieces of paper with cheerful messages on random seats when I knew the class following mine was to be taken by a mean teacher. 'Don't worry, it's nearly lunchtime!' I sometimes wrote. Or 'You are lovely. Think about what you are going to do this weekend.' There was a certain teacher who had a knack for intercepting any note passed round in class. He once found one of mine and as he opened it he smiled and said 'A good one for a change!' That made me smile too, and I liked the fact that he didn't know it was written by me. By the time I was thirteen or fourteen, I was leaving notes farther afield – stuck down the sides of bus seats or left on tables in fast-food restaurants. I felt like a secret good Samaritan, cheering people up on their way to work. To this day there must be hundreds of tiny bits of paper, covered in my curly teenage writing, very grubby and old by now and probably sandwiched between sweet wrappers and dried-out pieces of chewing gum, endlessly travelling the streets of Birmingham on clapped-out old buses.

I was growing up and could see that my mum had been dealt quite a difficult hand of cards in life. Her mother had died young, my dad had proved hopeless, she had a lot of kids to look after – including my brother, Jake, who had been diagnosed with autism and dyspraxia – and she had very little money to keep us all on. Despite her worries she didn't allow things to get on top of her; she kept going, day in, day out, and managed to be loving and fun at the same time. I always wanted to remind my mum how amazing she is so I'd leave her notes on the fridge or stuck on the TV for her to come downstairs to in the morning. When Ian's kids were staying, sometimes I'd get up early with little Kyle, letting everyone else sleep, and I'd sit writing a note for Mum while Kyle watched kids' TV. And when I was old enough to have a mobile phone I'd send Mum texts to show her I was thinking about her, and that she was loved.

♥

Life got quite tough in my mid-teens. Granddad had been ill for a while with cancer and when I was thirteen he died. My brother and I were pulled out of our Friday night youth club to say our goodbyes but by the time we got to Granddad's house he had passed away in bed. I asked if I could go and sit with him for a while, and I sat and talked to him on my own. I told him how much I was going to miss him, how I'd make him proud and how

44

I'd look after Mum at his funeral and sing a song he loved hearing me perform, a song called 'Count on Me' that Whitney Houston used to sing and which we both loved. Mum said throughout the day he had been looking into the corner of the room and speaking about my nanny. Some people believe that when you are dying you are greeted by the spirits of those you love. Many will shrug this off as rubbish, and that's fine. But when my granddad died he looked at peace, and he was smiling the kind of smile you have when you know everything is going to be OK.

I had felt secure and happy at secondary school, but after GCSEs I had to go to sixth-form college to do A levels as my school didn't have a sixth form. I found the move difficult; school had been a lovely, protected bubble whereas sixth form was a big change. There were three sixth-form colleges in the area, so my year was split up and I was separated from all my old friends. It was hard starting again and making new friends. I started dating a boy and things were going OK – nothing serious but quite fun – until one day one of his friends asked loudly why he was dating me when I was so fat. I'd never seen myself as fat before – I was a normal-sized kid – but it was as if this one thoughtless comment threw a switch in my head. All of a sudden I became obsessed with my weight, dieting, counting calories and fretting over portion sizes. The boyfriend was gone within a month – I quickly realised that he and his friends were a bunch of insecure arseholes – but unfortunately the obsession with my weight remained.

Most teenage girls go through a phase of worrying about their looks, thinking they are too fat or too spotty or their hair is the wrong colour or they don't like some part of their body. Most women still dislike something about their appearance. Lots are on diets way too often, but with luck and time they learn to live with their bodies, to dress in a way that brings out their best features and to avoid constantly thinking about their weight. That might have been me too, had I not met Tom.

I was sixteen and three quarters and though I'd had a fair few boyfriends, it had all been very innocent and I had never done much more than kiss. By this age, though, most of the girls in my class had had sex and I was starting to feel the pressure. When was I going to do 'it', and who would it be with?

Whoever it was with, I knew it was going to be wonderful. I was in love with the idea of love. I was a total romantic who had watched loads of soppy films and still cherished the memory of Nanny and Granddad's long and happy marriage. I wanted all that. I definitely didn't want to end up like my poor mum, with a no-good father for my kids.

There was quite a big alternative subculture in Birmingham, which a few people at my sixth-form college were into. My friend Aliss used to go to a club night for people into punk, rock and heavy metal music. We shouldn't have been there because we were too young. Each week we'd make up elaborate tales to tell the bouncers – one week we said it was my hen do, even though I was only sixteen. We were brought on stage and given cheap champagne to toast my imaginary celebration, which we found hilarious. Each week our stories got more elaborate and before long we were being ushered to the front of the queue by the bouncers. It was a lot of fun.

At this point I was a real 'emo'. Although at the time I wouldn't have admitted it out loud, I was the epitome of that kind of grunge music fan. I had black and blonde hair extensions, wore Converse sneakers and lashings of eyeliner, and I listened to bands such as Fall Out Boy, Alkaline Trio, Brand New and Taking Back Sunday – I still have a massive soft spot for all of them. Boys with floppy fringes and awkward stances, pretty eyes and tattoos were my biggest downfall. And this all started with Tom.

He was older than me, 23 in fact, and seemed a lot more mature. A mutual friend introduced us in a night-club. He was tall and hairy, and our friend warned me not to get interested in him because he was a ladies' man, that he wasn't looking for a girlfriend – so of course I was immediately keen. I wanted to be the girl who changed all that.

It was very romantic, exactly like in the films. We dated and he asked me to be his girlfriend via MSN messenger video chat, holding signs up to the screen on lots of pieces of card.

YOU ARE
SO PRETTY
AND LOVELY
WILL YOU
BE MY GIRLFRIEND?

I was blown away by this adorable gesture.

When I went to his house he was playing one of my favourite bands, Sigur Rós. This is exactly how every teen rom-com sex scene started, in my opinion. I'd talked myself into being ready and here it was happening.

We had sex, and it wasn't at all what I expected it to be. It was quick and boring and I wasn't really involved at all. I'd imagined something that was a patchwork of my favourite romantic comedies and bits of my friends' stories. I just wanted it to matter and this didn't feel as if it did. By the end of it I didn't feel as if I mattered to him. He had done it a bunch of times and knew I hadn't, so I thought he might show me the ropes, give me some sort of direction, but with that thought it was over. As he got dressed, I felt disposed of. This bit wasn't spoken about in toilet cubicles amongst giggles. This was the bit that left marks way deeper, silent ones that would be carried way longer than our encounter lasted. I felt as if I'd just allowed myself to be beaten up.

I told Mum the next morning. I passed her a note, which was sometimes our way of communicating difficult things as well as good ones. It read:

'Guess what happened?'

'What?' she wrote back.

'Me and Tom had sex.' The note wasn't scribbled with excitement, more as a confession. I felt as if I'd done something wrong.

Mum looked devastated. She knew he was older and where we had met, she knew I was struggling with food, skipping meals and counting calories, and she knew this wasn't the right time for me to be experimenting with such important things. Mum could see that I had become very introverted, finding it hard to go to college, and the only people I was close to were her and my best friend Aliss. Of all the things I could have done at that point in my life, I couldn't have chosen worse.

He dumped me later that day by text message. A long one, spanning many messages. Each one I'd read and have to delete, because my inbox only held around fourteen messages. So being dumped lasted about fifteen minutes. It was a dramatic message, quoting various songs by Damien Rice and using 'it's not you, it's me' clichés, to try to hide the fact he was an utter loser.

I had built Tom up in my head to be this amazing guy and had fallen completely head over heels with the idea of him. I thought he was going to be the man who rode in on a white horse to save me. However, I quickly learnt that when you feel you need saving is when you look in completely the wrong direction. I was left with my first experience of a broken heart.

I had already got into a cycle of controlling what I ate, counting calories and checking portion sizes after that first boy's comment about me being fat. But it got much worse now. I started to make myself vomit.

The first time it happened we had been out with friends for pizza, which I hadn't wanted to eat because it was stodgy and filling and had too many calories. I felt heavy afterwards, and all the way home I thought 'I must get it out'. So as soon as I got in I made myself sick. I felt empty. It took the spotlight off me hating myself for a minute (although now I can see it was all just part of the same problem). I felt as if by throwing up I was taking active steps to making myself look better.

After that I realised that I didn't need to count calories. I could eat normally and then make myself throw up. I thought I was clever: I would vomit and no-one would know, so there would be no more comments about what I had or hadn't eaten. I knew Mum had noticed my behaviour around food and I thought that this way I could diet and she wouldn't know. I liked doing it because it was mine, my secret. I lost weight – maybe a stone and a half – and looked ill and tired, but not thin. The strange thing was that I had always condemned this kind of behaviour. I knew I shouldn't do it. I had always been the good kid but now I was doing something I knew I shouldn't. I was rebelling, but it wasn't a rebellion against Mum; it was a weapon to hurt myself with. I became very self-involved and everyone else blurred out.

I was bulimic, as I've learned to call the condition, for several years. At the height of it I was making myself sick ten times a day, sometimes until I passed out. I had a ritual around it all, and somehow, in a weird and unhealthy way, the ritual made things feel better. I would eat then straight after eating I would go to the toilet and make myself sick, kidding myself that no-one had noticed. I even ate things that I knew wouldn't taste too bad when they came up again – sugary cereal was my food of choice. I genuinely thought I was so hideous I couldn't interact with other people. I would eat by myself in the garden, in the dogs' bed, anywhere I could get away from everyone else. Other people looking at me would see a very normal-looking seventeen-year-old girl, but when I looked in the mirror I saw someone morbidly obese. It wasn't rational, but then it wasn't really about my weight. I just couldn't cope with life and the bulimia was a control issue. It was something to focus on that distracted me from all my other problems. Many of which were just the normal problems every teenager goes through. My confidence was at rock bottom. It was as if someone had switched off a light inside me. My life felt out of control; I was in a new world which felt very threatening and my weight was the only thing I could control. With hindsight, I can see that I was never in control of the condition – the condition was in control of me. I wore my heart on my sleeve and didn't know how to protect myself from people who were unkind. Bulimia became my shield, even though it was beginning to destroy me from the inside.

My family cottoned on very quickly, of course. My breath smelt bad, I went to the toilet straight after eating and I kept passing out. It would have been hard to miss the signs. Maybe I didn't want the signs to be missed – maybe I wanted Mum to find out and rescue me. I hated myself and found it very difficult to ask for help, because I didn't think I deserved it. I had been rejected a lot – by my dad, by bullies at school, by crappy men. Even Granddad dying had felt like a kind of rejection. I had drawn the conclusion that the fewer people you were close to, the fewer could hurt you. So it was really just Mum and my best friend whom I trusted.

No-one said anything for a while but Mum stopped buying sugary cereal and started following me around the house a lot. Meals became a race to see who would finish first. Ian would bolt down his food then rush to sit in the bathroom for twenty minutes so that I couldn't get in there and throw up my food. One day I confessed what I was doing to Mum, who had been waiting for just that moment. She took me straight to the doctor and I started seeing specialists. One nutritionist warned me that I was weakening my heart, and that made me stop and think.

Thankfully I had a supportive family and an amazing doctor who got me through it. Dr Khan was a tall man of Egyptian heritage. His skin was golden, and he was very slim with long limbs and a voice that reassured you instantly. We just talked during the sessions, and it was almost as though he was part of my family. He didn't shout or get angry, but was calm and extremely rational without being patronising. The worst thing someone can do when you are in a bulimia cycle is to deem it stupid. To me, at that moment, it was absolutely everything. My life revolved around the ritual, and anyone who didn't understand was just someone else to distance myself from. I didn't think Dr Khan would judge me or think me ridiculous. He told me why I was feeling what I was feeling. He explained that my behaviour was addictive. That I had found something to damage myself with and was clinging to it. That I was set to self-destruct.

The bulimia went on for a few years. What Dr Khan eventually did to stop me being sick was to train me to imagine his face in the toilet bowl. Initially this terrified me, as I had once watched a documentary about pest control in which there was a scare story about a rat that climbed up the pipes and took a big chunk out of someone's bum while they were on the toilet. It was probably a made-up story but it has haunted my bathroom visits ever since. Seeing anybody's face in the toilet bowl would be possibly the scariest situation ever but seeing Dr Khan's lovely face – well, it would be rude to throw up all over it. So that finally stopped me. I went on seeing Dr Khan for years, until he left to go and work in A&E. I cried when he left. He had been my anchor since I was sixteen.

Doctors always think I became bulimic because I felt rejected by my dad. That's a tidy explanation, and there's probably some truth in it, but I'm not so sure. I think it's more that I've always been a very open person, who assumes people will be kind, so when they aren't – when people say hurtful, bullying things – it leaves me vulnerable. I hadn't yet learned how to keep your heart open but protect it at the same time: to recognise that when people say nasty things about you, it's usually because they feel bad about themselves and want to get rid of those bad feelings by passing them on to someone else. Someone they perceive as weaker than them. That's what bullying is about.

Bulimia never really leaves you. It's like depression in that way: once it has visited you it's always there, in the background, and it can always return. You just learn to control it and know when the thoughts of vomiting come along it's down to feeling out of control or stressed out, not because it's something you need to do.

What I do know is that the whole experience made me stronger. I believe in the saying 'what doesn't kill you makes you stronger'. I know it's possible to overcome even very big problems in life, to heal yourself and move on. And that's something I want to help other people understand.

♥

I left school at eighteen and started working. I have always been a workaholic – I collect jobs the way some people collect stamps or pet fish. By the time I was twenty I had three jobs: I was a waitress in a strip club, a barmaid in a pub, and I sold jewellery in a little shop called Beadasaurus. I didn't like the strip club at all. I didn't know it was going to be a strip club when I answered an advert on Gumtree for bar work, but when I turned up they gave me a uniform of heels – which I never normally wear – and sequinned hot pants, and put me straight on a shift. The club was full of footballers and big businessmen and the strippers ranged from girls paying their way through uni to women my mum's age. It was horrible. I saw such vile things there, it really made me feel dirty, but I still went every day because I needed the money. What with that and my other jobs, some days I had to work from 10am till 5am the following morning, but it didn't matter. I wanted to keep working, to earn money and to give me something positive to focus on.

The year before the tick bite I was working at a Levi's shop during the day and The Hare and Hounds pub at night. I liked both jobs and had close, supportive friends there so they became a massive part of my social life. I was always put in the ladies' department at Levi's because of my nature and the way I approached women. Buying jeans is an absolute nightmare for nearly every woman I've ever known. Getting the right fit is key and I wanted every customer to feel comfortable and beautiful. With all my experience of hating the way I looked I could completely relate to the women in the shop and any hang-ups they had about their bodies. Letters praising my customer service were sent to head office. It was great to be recognised for doing something well, since up to that point I had been expecting to be sacked because I couldn't fold T-shirts properly. I would come up with ways of doing it that I thought were artistic but were not the 'correct' way. Every day I was sure my boss would come over and say 'Hey, Picasso, you're sacked!' I do this in many aspects of my life: worry myself into a black hole. I think it's a family trait. Natural born worriers, us Bickleys.

The Hare and Hounds was more like a family – a massive dysfunctional family. Everyone who worked there was a little off the wall. There were the annoying younger brothers, the bossy parent types and the sisters who would bicker and love each other in equal measure. It was always fun to be at work; we were a team and we all had our roles.

When I wasn't at work, I was writing poetry, which I had rediscovered after I left college. Writing had become a brilliant outlet for me. I poured all my thoughts and feelings into my poems, and found being creative very comforting and fulfilling. I had a lot of adventures in love, and many of my poems revolved around that. One of them was about a guy called Tim who was kind of a local playboy. Like me, he was massively insecure so hid behind sex and getting absolutely smashed. He wasn't particularly attractive – I hadn't even noticed him before the night we got together – but he had an air of arrogance and charm that was really endearing. We slept together and I hoped it might turn into a few dates, but to Tim I was just another notch on his bedpost. I didn't like being just another notch so I decided to do something about it.

I still had problems with low self-esteem and not liking my body, but I had developed enough confidence through writing poetry to feel I had a way of getting back at Tim for using me. I'd learned about performance poetry – basically reciting it like song lyrics, in front of a crowd – so once I'd written a poem about Tim, my friends recorded me performing it and I put it up on Myspace. The poem was called 'On Call', the title of a song Tim liked by Kings of Leon, and he had a tattoo on his chest saying 'On Call', so was easily identifiable. News of the poem spread fast. It was ace. Other girls Tim had slept with messaged me saying 'At last!' Some friends of mine held a festival in their back garden, which I knew Tim was going to, so that was my opportunity. I performed the poem live there to an audience of about forty people.

On Call

Babe, look, I like you just not to that extent.

Um, then, what was the other night supposed to have
  meant?

*Look baby girl, you know how we roll. My bed has seen
  more than Ashley Cole's.*

Oh. I thought you were different.

Nah, we are all the same.

If you can't handle it, babe, don't play the game.

I'll play you a song and I'll give you the eye...

But if you want to see me more than once?

B-Y-E Byeee.

I haven't got commitment issues,

I've just got too much choice to stick around.

*How can I charm all these ladies, with my hands so tightly
  bound?*

If you want me to chase you,

I'm definitely not one to crawl –

You've seen the badge on my chest, right?

I'm always going to be 'on call'.

*Look, you are lovely, but there are too many fish in the
  sea –*

and they all need a good chance of getting it on with me.
I need to appear available and a girl will only cramp my
style.
But, look, can we make it so the air between us isn't hostile?
You've got some pretty fit friends and I'll probably get with
them one day.
Don't need any dirty looks you're giving sending drama
my way,
I didn't come with a contract, it was just a one night only.
Sorry if you read into it too much and feel a little lonely.
No, no, you're right – go back to your rock and roll
queens,
However, don't be complaining when your willy starts
going green.

Everybody loved it – apart from Tim. He came up to
me afterwards with his tail between his legs. 'You got me,'
he said sheepishly. I hear he swiftly got his tattoo covered
up.

I was so proud of myself for that night. I was shaking
with nerves, but I wanted people to hear my poem so I
got through the fear. I could have been depressed about
his behaviour but instead I turned it into something funny,
and I loved doing that. It felt good. I had always known
that words were powerful things. Now I was learning that
my words could be powerful too.

That same day I got an email from the Roundhouse

in Camden Town, London, asking me to take part in their poetry slam. I'd entered on a whim after Laura Dockrill, one of the only performance poets I'd ever really listened to, told me to give it a shot after I sent her some of my poems. I had no idea what a slam was. By the time I got there I was surrounded by a lot of people who definitely did, and I was the only one with a Brummie accent. Bar one named Polarbear. He was apparently quite a big deal and he was hosting. I didn't realise I would have to get up in front of over a hundred people and read my poems from my battered notebook. I trembled and shook through the first round, made it to the second, and somehow won. There are always a few days in life you can pinpoint as the start of a new chapter. That day was definitely one of them.

After that difficult period at sixth-form college, my life seemed to be back on track. I had a fantastic few years performing, working and hanging out with friends. I was full of energy and excitement, always busy, and I finally reached my target weight in 2011 – in a healthy way! There were lots of boys around, but I knew I'd met someone special when I got together with Wil. Wil and I started talking because someone had posted a film of me performing on his Facebook page. His first comment was 'I'm going to marry that girl'. I didn't know this when he friended me on Facebook and sent me a nice message saying that he liked my stuff. This wasn't the first time a stranger had got in touch online, so I didn't take much notice at first.

Wil was from Cromer, in Norfolk, which is quite a distance from Birmingham, but we started chatting online and didn't stop. From his photos he looked like a lot of fun, and I knew I wanted to get to know him. He was everything I had ever found attractive in a guy: dark hair, tattoos, piercings, and a year-round glow. I didn't think we would actually meet in real life because I wasn't the sort to meet people off the Internet and I had watched way too much real-crime TV to consider travelling anywhere alone. So I just got on with life. But I was growing fonder of this man I had never met and learning a lot about him through hours of talking via Facebook, Skyping and long telephone conversations.

Before my 23rd birthday, Wil said he was going to make me something. On the morning of my birthday I found a package from him on my doorstep with a handmade wooden earring inside. It was absolutely gorgeous and had obviously taken a lot of time and effort. I couldn't quite believe someone had spent that much time making something for me.

It was early August 2011, and I was at work on the till in Levi's when Wil walked in with some of his friends. I don't think I have ever been happier to see another person. In the flesh he was just so handsome, with the most beautiful eyes and smile. If I could pinpoint the moment

I started to fall in love, that was it. As soon as I finished on the till I threw my arms around him and kissed him. Wil's friends were wonderful; the type of people I could see myself getting on with really well.

Let me tell you about him! He was tall, with broad shoulders and big brown eyes that would disarm you at first sight. His body was an etch-a-sketch of trial and error tattoos. Some were beautiful while others, he would be the first to admit, had been ill-advised. I soon found he was one of the most talented people I had ever known, an insane artist and craftsman who made origami and intricate pieces of jewellery (like my earring), and could pick up new skills incredibly quickly. After a meal in a restaurant he would often leave a beautiful piece of origami, ranging from hearts to swans, for the waitress while, inspired by him, I would write her a thank-you note. Wil had a sense of fun like nobody I had ever known. His flamboyant personality was infectious and his striking good looks meant he was a hit with women of all ages. He was always trying to make people smile.

Wil went through fads, avidly collecting things for a few weeks at a time: a trumpet he swore he would learn one day; a bunch of rubber ducks. I never quite understood the motive behind the rubber ducks but became quite fond of them.

After that first surprise visit I was smitten. I went to Cromer for the weekend and Wil had planned the perfect visit: we had a picnic, went to the zoo, I met more of his friends and then soon I met Wil's family, who were amazing. We'd only known each other for a month but it became harder and harder to be apart, because we were caught up in such a whirlwind romance. We invented the perfect fantasy life for ourselves, living by the seaside, our children playing with wooden toys Wil had made for them while we grew vegetables in our back garden and kept hens. He was a complete romantic, always armed with a camera so that we would be able to remember the wonderful times we'd had when we were old and grey.

Meanwhile, by September 2011 I had already performed my poems at Glastonbury and Shambala, but I still couldn't believe my luck that I got to perform at all these legendary venues. Every new stage was an experience, whether it was a good one or not. I knew whatever I was after was down this road; I wasn't sure when or where I would find it but writing made me happier than I had ever been. When something makes you happy, you hold onto it, so I took up every offer to perform. Even if it meant me doing a six-hour round-trip for free in order to appear on stage at a festival, I would do it. I felt like a baby rock star, even if I was a rock star nobody recognised, skint and lost in a field of muddy tents. I loved every minute of it; I was the happiest girl. Everything had come together for me at last, and I loved being a grown-up, being free. I missed Wil when we weren't together, but we texted and called each other a lot.

Then I was invited to Bestival and I was so excited. I had always wanted to go to Bestival on the Isle of Wight, and getting to perform there was an absolute dream. One of my best friends, Sarah, and I shimmied ourselves over and pitched our tent. We aimed one day to have one of those big teepees that the artists who want to 'experience' the festival have. They are massive, big enough to stand up and run around in. I'm not sure that we'd actually run around, but it's always nice to have the option. A lot of the friends I had met through poetry were performing too so it was like a mini holiday. The weather was gorgeous, and I could not have had a better time. I was performing poetry in a forest by day to people lying in hammocks, and listening to Björk and The Maccabees by night. Sarah and I were absolute scamps, always armed with little bottles of concoctions we had made in the tent. Neither of us are heavy drinkers so a couple of sips would take us just where we needed to be: tipsy and mischievous.

We had a riot, and came home gloriously happy, sunburned and covered with insect bites. If I had a box big enough I would have stuffed every last second of that summer into it. We had had an adventure … but the adventure would soon lead to a nightmare.

Chapter four
I asked Mum if I was going to die.

18 December 2011

A Nurse
Solihull Hospital
Lode Lane
Solihull
B91 2JL

Dear Nurse (I'm sorry, I can't even remember your name),

This is for you but even if you read this letter I doubt you'll realise it's about you. I doubt your actions that night in your mind would have ever been worth writing about - but they were. You are worth writing about over and over.

I was so scared. I'm not sure whether it was the amount of morphine running through my veins or the fact that I had never needed my mum more. Everything was out of control, the world was spinning too fast and the only thing I could think about was worrying whether I'd

just slept funny and was causing a fuss about nothing.
For about twenty minutes I cried out, afraid and exhausted
and embarrassed for crying, whilst you held my hand. You
didn't tell me it was all going to be OK. I didn't need
that - I just needed somebody to be there. When you
thought I'd gone to sleep you kissed my forehead. I'm
pretty sure you didn't have to do that but you did and it
made all the difference.
Thank you.
Jodi
Xx

A lot of my memories from hospital are hazy, mainly
because I was on so much morphine and other drugs
to cope with the pain. I woke up properly on day three
on a general ward, in the bed right by the nurses' station
because I needed a bit more TLC. Little bits of conversations I'd overheard were coming back to me. I was in the
state of consciousness where you are awake but simply
do not have the energy to open your eyes. I was hooked
up to a machine with various fluids going into my arm
– anti-viral medicine and antibiotics, I found out later.
Who knew that being seriously ill felt like you were made
of fondue and marshmallows?

I remembered my brain was worrying the doctors
and when my mum came in she and a nurse explained
to me that the doctors thought I had contracted

meningoencephalitis from a tick bite. It was a very rare viral infection, which could be fatal. Encephalitis means swelling of the brain.

They didn't tell me much else about the infection other than that the doctors thought they had caught it relatively fast. Thankfully, I was over the worst. Wil came down from Norfolk to be with me. My brother Jake didn't say much, but sometimes with Jake you have to accept that him being there says more than any words.

I wasn't fully awake and it took me ages to take it all in. Mum gave it to me in bursts as I drifted in and out of sleep. When I woke up for any length of time the big questions started to go round and round in my mind in a frightening loop. Is this a forever thing? Will it be different tomorrow? What's going to happen next? Could it get any worse? But I didn't have any of the answers and neither did the doctors. I remember asking my mum that first night if I was going to die. She said 'no', in a way I now realise meant 'You are going to survive even if I have to give you every last one of my vital organs.'

There was so much to take on board. People kept using scary terms like 'brain infection' and 'lumbar puncture', which I knew I'd had when I was admitted to ease the pressure on my brain. There were loads of nurses around me, and I knew I was on morphine which meant it had to be very serious. I was very confused, and extremely frightened.

That night I was woken up by a doctor scratching my feet with the bottom of a pen. This wasn't a strange form of torture but a medical test I came to know well. He was checking to see what I could and couldn't feel. My left side was fine but I couldn't feel the right side. The doctor tried to get me up to do some more neurological tests, but I couldn't stand. There were mumbles about the infection having brought on a TIA, which is a mini-stroke. I didn't like the sound of that at all. To avoid putting the fear in me any further the doctor left me to sleep, saying he would check on me in the morning. I lay on my back, freaking out, pinching and punching my right arm until it was covered with red marks. I hoped one of the blows would really, really hurt, to prove that I was just imagining it. But the punches didn't hurt. I didn't feel a thing.

With my left hand I grabbed a pen and notebook from the bedside table. I tried to write with my right hand but couldn't manage it. It looked as if a three-year-old had been let loose with a felt-tip. It was nothing like adult writing. I know people use the expression 'my heart sank' too much, but at that moment I genuinely felt my heart sink into my stomach. Nothing seemed fair and I was terrified. We often complain about stuff that's not very important, and I so wanted this not to be important – but it was. I kept telling myself that it could be worse, that I was alive, that it's all relative, but there was no getting away from it. No amount of looking on the bright side was going to fix this one. Right now, no matter how many bad things were going on in the world outside, my world, which I had carefully built after several difficult years, had just fallen apart. And I was alone.

I wasn't alone, though. There were a lot of other people in that hospital, even if they were all strangers, and many of them were as scared as I was. It was 2am, and I strongly identified with the man down the hall who was convinced we were in prison and kept ringing the alarm for the nurses throughout the night as if to say 'Don't you dare forget about me!' I was in fear of disappearing too when the nurse came over. I'd spotted her earlier when Mum was here. She was tall and plump with a ball of grey hair and tattoos on her wrist, which in that moment I clung to as if we were soul sisters. I must have looked desperate because she moved a chair nearer to my bed, sat down and waited quietly while I cried. She didn't say anything, just sat there with me while I cried, and that was what I needed. Then she kissed me on my forehead like Mum always did, and that must have sent me off to sleep.

The next morning I woke up to a ring of doctors around my bed. You'd think I'd have had better things to worry about, given that I had nearly died a couple of days earlier, but my initial thought was 'I have not washed in four days. If they want to do the feet test again I will have to refuse. Or die of shame.' Dread filled me, just like the time I was six and was terrified of my teacher because she was horrid, so instead of asking to go to the toilet I did a wee all over the mat. The doctors did do the feet test again and were very polite about my feet. Even though Mum said at one point that my feet and our dog's feet smelt exactly the same. All the doctors seemed pretty sure that a couple of days after I first got ill I'd had a mini-stroke, otherwise known as a TIA. A TIA occurs when a tiny blood clot prevents blood from getting to a part of the brain. The brain is only without oxygen for a few minutes and recovers quickly but it can cause temporary paralysis on one side of the body. It was all pretty scary. A stroke is something you're supposed to have when you're old, not when you're 23!

As time passed, the lack of feeling slowly turned into a dullness and the sensation started to return, but I still couldn't feel as much as usual on my right side. I stayed on that ward in Solihull Hospital for fifteen days. I had been in the hospital many times before. I was born there, had my appendix out there and had attended a lot of appointments for bulimia. The smell of disinfectant and overcooked food was the same. But this stay would be my longest yet. When I came around properly a few days later the ladies opposite me told me that when I came in they didn't think I would make it through the night. I guess it must have looked scary, with me pretty much unconscious and tubes going into my arm.

Once the strongest painkillers wore off I felt as if I had

been run over. My body didn't feel like my own and almost everything I tried to do reminded me that it wasn't working properly. My head ached constantly, with an awful, exhausting sort of pain. I would wake up in the morning to find breakfast on my bedside table, go to pick up the spoon with my right hand and drop it because I couldn't feel the spoon properly. I could see the spoon, so I knew it was in my hand, but I couldn't assess its weight or size, so pretty rapidly it fell out of my grip. My tea had to be drunk cold in case I dropped the cup on myself. And I still couldn't hold a pen. I would get really upset so the nurses started hiding pens from me. They were doing it to be kind but I got frustrated and panicky about it. It felt a bit like my arm had been numbed by a local anaesthetic ready for a doctor to stick a big needle in it: not a knock-down-drag-out anaesthetic, because I could feel a degree of pressure, but nothing like the sensation you'd normally feel.

All the nurses were amazing. They would sit with me and talk about their families and boyfriends and anything they could think of to keep me smiling. The ward clerk, Janet, became one of my favourites. She was the person who made me realise that it is important to ask for help, that it isn't a sign of weakness. I've always been someone who fights battles on her own, so asking for help was difficult. Many of us, me included, think we don't deserve help, when of course we do. Everyone deserves to be

helped, especially when they are feeling poorly. We just
need to learn that it's OK to ask, that everyone is vulnerable sometimes. Janet would say 'Jodi, you are not here
for the fun of it. You have got to let us help. We want to
help you.' She said this over and over until it sank in.
Janet knew I would try to put on a brave face when big
groups of visitors came because I didn't want them to
fuss over me but after these visits I would be extra-
exhausted and poorly. Once Janet let me try to walk to
her (not far, she wasn't mean!) as a way of showing me
that I needed the nurses' help to get around and do things
that before had been so simple.

Walking was a massive problem. I was like Bambi on
ice. The link between my brain and my right leg was not
working at all well. Out of sheer stubbornness I would
try to shuffle across the ward, clinging onto furniture as
I went. I could sort of lurch from one fixed object to the
next, grabbing anything I could with my good hand. I
was constantly on the verge of falling but desperate to
avoid asking for help. My distinctive shuffle soon became
known as 'the Beyoncé', after the strongest, most independent woman ever, because I wiggled my bum as I
moved. Janet would shout 'Beyoncé is on the move!' and
the nurses would run to help me to the toilet or wherever
I was trying to go.

Another nurse I became really fond of was called
Andrew. He was very sarcastic and we shared banter that

came totally naturally and made a bad situation better. I've seen him since at appointments and he's still the same – bane of my life. But I love people like that, the ones who don't take life too seriously and just make the best of whatever is in front of them. We both understood that the situation I was in wasn't ideal but he made me laugh and took the piss out of me on the days I was up for it.

I was on a general ward, the 'clinical decision unit', sometimes known as the 'can't decide unit' – which has been the story of my illness, really – so there were all sorts of patients there. I was the youngest on the ward, and became very fond of some of the older female patients, who looked out for me. It was like having a load of grannies, and as I hadn't had one for ages that was lovely. I reckon if I had been the same age as these women we would have been the best of friends, and as it was we had a lot of laughter and shared jokes. Whilst in hospital we became each others' bit of sunshine in a scary place. We were all fragile for different reasons, but found comfort and support in each other. If I kept trying to do a certain thing I wasn't supposed to – such as get up out of bed or hold a pen – one of the ladies would have a word with a nurse so they could distract me. If the cleaner turned the bay lights on in the morning, someone would always turn them off for me because my eyes were hyper-sensitive to light.

Brenda was three beds away from me: a tiny lady, she

made the hospital chairs seem as if they were built for giants. She had dark curly hair that looked as if it only ever grew straight upwards, and a personality to match. She was fierce, hilarious and very sharp-witted. Brenda was dying of cancer, not that you'd know. She had tubes that she was supposed to attach to her nose way more often than she did. Her vices were exotic fruit teas and a brandy of a night-time. She missed her brandy on the ward. Brenda would always ask me if I was going dancing when I set off lurching around the ward, and she'd tell me off when I attempted to go it alone. She made me laugh, joking that it was the hospital food killing her, not the cancer. Brenda was a powerhouse, the kind of woman who held her family together – as shown by her crowded bedside at visiting times and the mass of sweets in her drawer. Though she was feisty, Brenda could also be quietly kind, rubbing my leg in a reassuring gesture as she passed my bed.

Margaret in the bed next to me was a chatterbox, which was what I needed. I wanted to hear everything she had to say as it took my mind off my own situation. Margaret was beautiful in the same way Helen Mirren is, with glittery eyes and bobbed hair in a shade of silver that girls my age try hard to achieve with various dye jobs but can never quite match. Margaret was opinionated, which displeased the nurses sometimes but I loved it. She told me about how she met her husband Terry. Margaret would go to the same café with her friends during her lunch break from work and Terry wandered in one day. She said she knew instantly he was going to turn her world upside down. She said that's what love is – the end of the world as you know it and the beginning of something a little bit more wonderful. I loved her romantic stories and when I met Terry for the first time I could put a face to all the descriptions she had given me. Margaret worried about how Terry was coping without her and every time he came to visit she would question his ability to look after himself, pointing out that he hadn't shaved or done a button up properly. She thought more about him than she did about herself. Margaret and Terry were in love in a way that I thought my nanny and granddad would have been too, had they still been alive. I saw in them what I hoped for in my own life. They were like teenagers, never letting go of each other's hand, sitting across a hospital table from one another, taking in every inch of the other's face as if to trace it deeper into memory until the next visiting time.

Margaret was my advocate when the doctors came on their rounds. She got angry with them and told them to sort me out because I was young and beautiful and had my whole life ahead of me. I felt very far from beautiful but it was nice to have her support. I was desperate for the doctors to sort me out too. It was all very frightening. The world had come back into focus but I still had a terrible headache and couldn't really feel my right side. Margaret often sat near me and held my hand as I fell asleep, like a mother by her child's bedside, even though she was plugged into an oxygen tank more often than not. Everyone needs to be touched; it's healing, and Brenda and Margaret knew it.

When elderly people pay you a compliment or comment on your character I think we tend to believe them a little more than we would someone our own age. Maybe because with age comes wisdom. Older people know what life can throw at you because they've had it thrown at them, and they know what matters most. When I was at my weakest Brenda told me I was strong and that I'd get through this, and I believed her. And that helped.

Sometimes people need to be told they are amazing, to drown out the negativity and the fear. Sometimes when someone else isn't feeling strong you need to be extra-strong for them. They need you to tell them that they can cope, they can get better, because so much of healing is about belief, about positivity and determination. Now I'm not one of those who thinks it's all in the mind – I'll take surgery and medicine every time. But the mind is important too, and Brenda and Margaret were strong for me.

My family was an absolute rock throughout my time in hospital. Mum has never been one for saying things like 'Oh poor you, it isn't fair'; that isn't in her nature.

She's one of life's doers instead. But she was there for me every day, every visiting hour. Mum battled for me, talking to the doctors, bringing me news and stories from the outside world, and bringing me food I'd loved as a child, like cheese and tomato pitta bread pizza. Ian and my brother Jake were there too, and so were my friends. One friend from the pub, Katie, even brought in Sunday lunch for me and Mum. We sat on the ward – me, my mum and my friend Katie – all three of us eating a roast dinner with all the trimmings from the pub's carvery.

Mum never allowed me to think I wouldn't get better. I have no doubt that she went home at the end of every day and broke her heart, but I think she found comfort in doing practical things for me. And I knew that every little thing she did for me was a sign of her love.

October came and the doctors still didn't seem to know exactly what had happened to me – or what my prospects were – but I was desperate to go home. Before I was discharged, the physiotherapist came to my bed to give me a zimmer frame. She was stern and spoke to me as if I had chosen not to walk, as if I was inconveniencing her. I didn't ask many questions because I just wanted to go home and get on with life. The doctors had told my mum that if she saw any deterioration in my condition she should bring me straight back to hospital, and that we shouldn't expect a miraculous recovery. They thought I would get better – how much better they didn't know –

and that my walking and writing would come back in due course. They never said how long 'in due course' might be. Much later I learned that recovery from encephalitis can take up to eighteen months. I don't know how I would have coped with that knowledge at the time. In my mind 'due course' meant a month or two. I said my goodbyes, was given a big bag full of painkillers and pushed off in a wheelchair.

It was wonderful to leave the hospital behind, to feel fresh air on my face again. The doctors and nurses all had my best interests at heart and were very kind to me but even so, it felt as if I had been released from prison. But I wasn't going to manage by myself at all. I was very weak, couldn't walk unaided and needed constant supervision. I still couldn't feel my right leg as well as I could feel the left; there was a massive difference in sensation. Everything that had come easily before I now needed help with, from getting dressed to showering. It was as if a toddler had taken over my controls.

I went back to my mum's house, and Wil moved in to help look after me. He had been incredible while I was in hospital, not only to me but to my mum, too. Every day on the ward I would wake up to presents from him – not bought, handmade. Mum told me that he would sit for hours in my bedroom at home, hand-crafting things to bring to the hospital the next day. He made me a sock teddy out of one of my socks, complete with button eyes and a smile. All these tiny, kind, thoughtful gestures made such a difference to the way I was feeling.

Now Wil and I were at my mum's together, sleeping on the living-room floor because the bathroom was on the ground floor and I couldn't manage the stairs. The house hadn't changed at all but most of my siblings had left, so it was just my mum, Ian, Jake and Danny. I didn't have to babysit the younger ones any longer; instead everyone was looking after me. It felt as if I was going backwards in life.

Wil and I had only been together for a month or so before I got poorly, and most of the time it had been a long-distance relationship. When we were suddenly thrown together day-in-day-out we began to learn that our knowledge of each other was pretty limited. We had spent no more than a handful of days together when I was well, and our whirlwind romance was threatening to blow itself out. In hindsight I can see that we had been in that giddy, slightly daft phase of a relationship where you ask each other questions like 'If you could either have a head so big you couldn't fit through doors or arms that were permanently up in the air, which would you choose?' (Wil would have a massive head.) The questions we didn't have the answers to were ones like 'Can you help rebuild my life?' and 'Will you be there for me in the bad times as well as the good?' We were too young to suspect that these kinds of answers would be needed. But all of a sudden they were. And we didn't really know each other at all.

Before I got ill I had signed the paperwork to rent a house with three friends from work. There had been talk of Wil moving in too, but now that I was ill it was a necessity rather than an idea. So in November 2011, soon after I was discharged from hospital, Wil and I moved from Mum's living-room floor to our rented place. I was still very wobbly, and spent most of the time in our bedroom with Wil. Much of the time I was in bed. The furthest I ventured in my wheelchair or on my zimmer frame was to the top of the road to top up the gas and electricity keys or to buy food. It was totally claustrophobic, just me and Wil in one room. I became extremely dependent on my mum coming to take me away from what felt like a prison cell. I needed air, even if it was just sitting in the car while she shopped. I wanted to feel a bit normal again.

At the time it really surprised me that Wil stuck around after I got ill. I will always have massive love and respect for him for doing that. It would have been easy for him to just cut his losses and walk away, especially as we were already in a long-distance relationship. If he had chosen to do so, I would obviously have been gutted but I would have understood. It was a lot to take on but Wil didn't move an inch. He didn't even wobble because in his mind I was going to get better, then we would get married and have children – and live the life we had dreamt up. As I began to get better, I found this harder and harder to take. I didn't like the life I had now. I wasn't sure whether that meant the life I had with Wil or my life post-encephalitis, but at that moment I couldn't differentiate between the two. Wil was right in the middle of this new world and I felt as if I was letting him down, cheating him almost; this wasn't what he signed up for.

I hated Wil seeing me ill. I was getting migraines that made me throw up, and Wil would have to take me to the toilet, which was humiliating. I wanted him to think I was pretty; I didn't want him having to hold my hair back and mop up vomit. I had started to put on weight again due to not being active and although this was the least of my problems it didn't help the way I felt about myself. The hatred I'd had for my body quickly returned. I remember one night in particular, we were both in bed and he had fallen asleep hugging me. I cried and cried, quietly and alone, because I knew I was pushing him away but there was nothing either of us could do about it. I was depressed, I was in pain, I didn't like my body any more and the illness, together with all the medicine I was on, meant I didn't have the energy or the desire to be intimate. Wil couldn't understand that; he thought it meant I didn't love him any more. Which was completely understandable. All he needed was some reassurance but sometimes I didn't even have the energy to kiss him. The more Wil tried to be close to me, the more I withdrew.

I knew that Wil would move heaven and earth for me, but I didn't want him to. I wanted to be normal. This wasn't normal, and everything was completely outside our control. Wil was in a horribly difficult situation because he had moved to Birmingham to be with me, but I was the only person he knew – so when I visited my mum to escape the room, he was left alone. I tried to introduce him to people but he didn't seem interested. I felt smothered, as if I were drowning. He no longer had any motivation to make things or even get dressed; I felt as if I had knocked all the life out of him. When we met we were both so full of life and love, we were better versions of ourselves, and now I felt I had ruined him. I felt I'd taken his spark away – or the situation we were in had; either way the guilt was awful.

I felt I had lost my identity. I couldn't work, I could hardly even go out, and I hated it. I had been fiercely independent and suddenly I needed Wil to do pretty much everything for me. I felt trapped, beholden to him and I started to see him as stopping me from moving forward and getting better. I felt my attitude towards him changing. I resented the fact that I needed him and every day I had to stop myself from pushing him away.

Even now I feel as though my condition can suck all the air out of a room, and that's why I try to make light of it a lot. Wil would never admit that it drained him to see me as ill as I was but it did. The emotional strain of caring for someone who is unwell is huge. People never asked how Wil was; they would only ask him how I was. Although he never complained, I could see that it was as if he was drowning too. He needed someone to tell him it was all going to be OK, but there wasn't anyone to do that. It wasn't just my life that had changed; so had Wil's and my family's, especially my mum's. Wil became withdrawn and lost a lot of weight. He had moved away from Norfolk and everything he had ever known to become … what? My boyfriend? Or my carer? He wouldn't go out because he saw looking after me as his exclusive responsibility. He put a lot of unreasonable demands on himself, which is a common issue amongst carers. When I slept, Wil would sleep. Looking after someone who is ill is exhausting, both physically and mentally.

I know better now, but at the time, in pain, frustrated and angry as I was, I became convinced that everyone was holding me back from my recovery, Wil in particular. I came to resent him bitterly. He felt like a burden rather than a help. We started to bicker, sitting next to each other for hours in our little bedroom but barely speaking. We were not the person each other had fallen in love with, through no fault of our own. Eventually, I went to stay at my mum's. I told him I wasn't happy any more, I didn't want to be looked after any more. We argued. The sort of argument you have when you have nothing left to lose. I thought he was controlling me, that he wanted to keep

me a prisoner, all to himself. Whereas his argument was
he only knew that house, our room, and he was struggling
with me trying to fight for independence that I wasn't
ready for. We shouted and cried, telling each other this
was not how it was all supposed to work out. But we
couldn't do anything about it. Wil went back to Cromer,
and that was it. It was over. For the first few days I felt
free – and then I felt so, so alone.

I had really believed that Wil and I would be together
forever, but the pressure of my illness put a stop to all
that. Just one shitty little tick bite – it was as if I'd tumbled
not only to the bottom of the mountain, but carried on
tumbling down the road and into a ditch.

Dear Wil,

I've written this letter to you so many times. I'm never
really sure what to write - but for a while I felt like
something had been left unsaid. I was trying to find you an
explanation for something that neither of us had control of.
Some days I feel I still owe you that. You deserve something for all you went through. That isn't meant to sound
patronising and I hope you don't read it that way. What I
mean is if I could orchestrate some way of sorting events
or the planets to lead to you having the happiest life ever,
I would do that. I could fill your world with thank-you notes
and it wouldn't be enough to tell you how grateful I am for
you being with me through the bad days.

You taught me how to laugh at myself, properly. I've always laughed at myself but whilst laughing every other part of me is blushing red with embarrassment. On the days I didn't have the energy to put my bra on, thank you for putting it on backwards. Thank you for dancing with me when my walking resembled a drunk attempting to cha-cha. On the days when I fell over in Mum's living room and convinced myself I should stop even trying to walk, you were my legs and my arms and my positivity and my energy. You trusted me with every last piece of you and I felt I had nothing to give back. I felt I was just a shadow of someone I knew once. I was waking up with someone I loved but hadn't got the chance to know, and meanwhile I was disappearing by the second. We spent most days in one room, and moments of silence became hours.

When I started feeling a little better I clawed at every inch of independence I could get. I would try and escape that room and whether you were with me or not became less and less of a concern. I was desperate for normality. There wasn't enough air in that room for both of us any more. I am so sorry about that. I believe we leave bits of our heart with those we love and I'm sure a chunk of mine is left in the Cromer sand.

I wish you every last bit of happiness.

Jodi

X

Chapter five
I didn't know who I was anymore.

To Mum and Jake,

When I was little, Mum, I would trace pictures on your arms - using your freckles as a giant dot to dot. I remember being very small when I first wished for as many freckles as you. By eleven I had a bunch and hated them. They were huge brown spots on skin I had yet to grow into and I just wanted rid of them all. You stood in the porch and said 'You will never be able to grasp your wonder, every inch of you, every freckle - leave that to those who love you.' I have always felt loved. You've made sure of that. Love alone has healed so much in our household. Although all three of us bear scars of prior battles we are the strongest of armies. We learnt that home isn't only where the heart is, it's wherever you are, Mum. Wherever we have ended up, whatever we have landed ourselves in - you have brought love, patience and immeasurable kindness. Always. I can speak for us both, when I say you'll never know just how grateful we are.

And to Jake, you'll never truly know how proud I am of

you. It's not a textbook version of why one person should be proud of another, it's complicated. We are both so complicated, but I love every last tangle and knot of you. You impress and terrify me in equal measure; the things you do that make me want to write your name on every rooftop are on a par with those that make me want to slap you hard around the head. You are so much better than you know.

Go, team!

You will never be able to grasp how amazing you are.

Thank you, for everything.

Love, always.

Jodi xx

I t's hard, as an adult, to ask for anything. To be dependent on other people. I guess we all wish we were tough little cactus plants: needing the occasional bit of water but on the whole completely independent, able to protect ourselves when need be. I wanted to be a cactus. I wanted nothing more than to grow spikes and root myself in the ground. Sadly, the reality was that I couldn't stand on my own for long enough to even think about rooting anywhere. And the closest I was getting to spikes was my unshaven legs. I really didn't feel OK about any of the things that were happening to me and the feeling of powerlessness was awful. I hated being so dependent on other people's goodwill. I felt I'd lost myself and I was angry. The frustration of being poorly would make me break down and I would find myself sobbing in my mum's arms, again and again.

In the long, painful months after falling ill I felt as if I was in mourning. That sounds melodramatic, I know, but I honestly felt as if I had lost everything I'd accomplished so far. For example, after years of struggling, by the summer of 2011 I had finally lost three stone and got to a healthy weight by eating well, working two jobs, and generally just being a busy bee, on my feet the whole time. I was extremely proud of myself and for the first time in years felt happy with my body. But then I got ill, and while I was in hospital, at first unconscious and then unable to hop, skip and jump around the ward, I regained a lot of weight. This left me feeling not very cute. I also looked and felt like the walking dead from being ill and had as much energy as a sloth with a hangover. And I had just broken up with the guy I'd thought would be the love of my life. I felt really glum, as if someone had switched off a light inside me.

With hindsight, I can see that I was bound to feel miserable after all that had happened to me, but when you're in a bad patch you feel as if it will never end. It will, but you can't see it at the time.

I couldn't work, though I was stubborn enough to want to try. I asked both bosses – at the jeans shop and at the pub – if I could come back to work the following week (which, of course, I couldn't as I couldn't even walk to work, never mind do the jobs). Thankfully they both said 'No way!' It was hard realising how important being busy had been to me. I still couldn't function by myself or do any of the things I had always taken for granted. Most of us are used to being able to open the front door and step out by ourselves, without even thinking about it. And now I couldn't. I had no freedom; I was trapped in my own body. One day I tried to talk on the phone and get dressed at the same time. In the past I'd been Queen of this kind of multi-tasking, but now I ended up with half a bra on, tangled up in one trouser leg, lying on the floor. Mum found me lying there, crying, not long after.

Every day was the same, week after week. The whole waking up and hoping it's a dream thing? That happens. Waking up every day wishing things were different, worrying about the future, about what might happen. Would I ever get better? Would I have a headache for the rest of my life? Would I learn to walk and write normally again? How would I be able to support myself? What would I do for money if I couldn't work? Would I ever fall in love again? Could I find a new relationship? Who would want an invalid like me? And what about having children one day? Would that even be possible now? All this worry and uncertainty was draining and dragging myself out of it was hard. When I was suffering from heartbreak or bulimia, I had been able to tell myself that

94

it wouldn't be like this for long, that the situation would pass, that time would heal, and slowly, I would start to believe that message and things would change. But this was different because now my condition really was beyond my control. I had to find new ways of living. Other, smaller things to look forward to.

My family helped all they could. Jake would walk me up the stairs and come down on his bum with me. This was something my mum came up with after the morning when I felt brave and tried to walk down the stairs by myself, but ended up with a fat lip after falling. Jake or Mum would sit in front of me, I wrapped my legs around them, and we would bump down the stairs. This was something we had done as kids and gave us a lot of laughs. Just for a moment, we were able to imagine ourselves back in more carefree times, when the house was our adventure playground and going bump, bump, bump down the stairs on your bottom was all it took to make us smile. You have to make light of little things like that because it makes the big setbacks feel less threatening. My family has always been really good at turning crisis into comedy. I wasn't left alone often, which was good, because on my own I would either injure myself trying to do too much, or I would think too much. Both equally destructive.

I really needed to get back to normal but my first physiotherapy session wasn't until two and a half months after I was discharged from hospital. It was my first hospital appointment with a therapist since my illness and I felt resentful even at the outset. Two and a half months was too long to wait. I wasn't in the mood for this appointment. I went in with an attitude, feeling I'd had to help myself while the hospital had just left me to get on with it. The physiotherapist I had seen in hospital hadn't helped at all.

My new physiotherapist was rotund with very short curly hair. She was a lot nicer than the first physio, but in a dinner-lady way. She spoke to me as if she was talking to a little kid, not an adult. She didn't mean to be patronising but kept saying things like 'Oh, it's going to be all right', when anyone could see that it wasn't all right and there was no reason to believe that it ever would be.

The room we were in was kitted out like a very basic gym. There were parallel bars I had to hold onto and walk up and down. I did the neurological tests, which I've done a million times now and know off by heart. First you hold your arms up in front of you, at the level of your head. If one of them sinks, the opposite side of your brain is weaker. My right arm was still lacking in strength. Then, lying down, you have to lift your legs up in the air and the doctor asks you to push against his or her hand to see if either side is lacking in strength. My right leg was lacking in strength. Then all the reflexes are checked to make sure your brain is responding correctly, which mine was. Last of all there is following the finger, touching your nose then the other person's finger. That I could do fine.

The physiotherapist explained that I needed to retrain my brain to remember how to walk again. She moved my head up and down and from one side to the other, which hurt my legs. It felt weird; I think it must have been because I was straining the muscles in my leg by not standing straight. I explained that I kept having headaches and that I needed to go back to work, but the physiotherapist chuckled to herself and murmured that would happen 'eventually'. It wasn't a good response. I needed something to cling to, something to build me up, something encouraging. Without any answers, or a time frame for recovery, I had nothing to hope for. She said it would improve at some point but I wanted it *now*.

I needed to walk again and realised I was going to have to learn by myself. You can't wait for things to happen to you; you have to put the wheels in motion. No-one is going to do it for you. Sometimes being stubborn is a good thing. I set myself small goals for each day and worked hard towards them. If I tried to climb a mountain during the day, I crashed. I quickly learned that small steps lead to more progress and less disappointment. That sometimes just opening my eyes and getting out of bed was as much of a success as it would have been hiking up Everest. When I was alone in my room upstairs I would do laps across the room and then around it, gradually balancing more and more on both legs till I felt confident. It was a bit like learning to roller-skate. My old room was the size of a matchbox – but it was all the space I needed. Any more and I'd have crashed. I knew poor Mum was downstairs, waiting for me to fall over with a big thud. She checked on me occasionally but mostly let me get on with it, reasoning that my room was so small I couldn't come to much harm.

I still had reduced sensation in my right leg, so I had to watch it and concentrate as I moved it, otherwise I would fall. My left leg was normal, so could sense exactly what my body weighed and could support it. My right leg couldn't assess the weight, which meant that it would wobble and I would fall. I learned to watch my leg as I moved it, really focus on it, and slowly the sensation came back and I relearned how to do it instinctively. I watched Beyoncé videos over and over, hoping that my legs would learn to work exactly like hers. And hopefully look like hers too.

When I thought I had cracked it I decided to show Mum. It was my big moment, and I was proud of the effort I had put in and what I had achieved. I got Mum to bump me downstairs to the living room on my bottom, then told her to go into the room and wait. I don't know what she thought I was planning, but she went along with it. Then I walked triumphantly into our living room by myself, zimmer frame cast aside, and promptly tripped over a tomato sauce bottle someone had left on the floor and fell. I didn't hurt myself, but I must have cried for about an hour with sheer frustration and disappointment. 'I'm never going to be able to do this!' I wailed. After a while I stopped crying and we started laughing. All our emotions were jumbled up together. But soon I could look on the bright side again. I had walked by myself, even if it wasn't exactly like Beyoncé, and without the silly sauce bottle I wouldn't have fallen. So it felt as if I turned a corner that day: I knew that I would be able to walk again, and that belief gave me a reason to keep trying.

There were a lot of setbacks. There always are, and it's important not to get too downcast about them – though that's easier said than done. So often it was the tiny things that opened the floodgates. My Mum often talks about 'peg days', after the day when we were kids and she dropped the basket of pegs for hanging up the washing so they spilled all over the floor, then spent the rest of the morning crying – much to my confusion. What did it matter that Mummy had dropped some wooden clothes pegs on the floor? It didn't matter at all. What did matter was that my nanny had died a few weeks before, my mum had tried to appear strong for us and then the pegs were just the final straw. In our family, a peg day is when someone has a very trivial accident and that releases all the pent-up sadness and frustration they have been feeling. I had a lot of peg days around this time.

It didn't help that when I went out with my zimmer frame people would stare and give me funny looks. One time, as I was leaving the Hare and Hounds, where Mum had taken me to see my friends and old boss, I came out on my zimmer frame and a group of lads outside laughed at me. I heard the laughter and looked up sharply to realise they were people I knew. The ashamed looks on their faces when they recognised me will stay with me for a long time. I'm not sure they would have felt ashamed if they hadn't known who I was, but because the object of their meanness suddenly had a familiar face I think it hit them just how unkind they had been.

I wanted to stop people and say 'Two months ago, I was you. You could easily be standing here with this zimmer frame instead of me.' But rather than getting into an argument, I used to fantasise about the different ways I could use my zimmer to destroy them, if all this pain was just my superhero powers making their way out. Mum stopped me getting too wound up by mean reactions. 'Don't let the arseholes grind you down,' she'd say, lifting my chin up every time. But the reactions stopped me going out in public with my zimmer frame for a while. I was proud, and my pride held me back.

As ever, my family and friends found a solution. My brother Jake and my friends adapted a theme tune for my travels, thanks to 1990s R&B sensation Beenie Man. 'Zim, Zimmer. Who's got the keys to my Beamer?' We sang it all the time, wherever I went, and it really helped. Humour is the best medicine. A couple of rounds of singing daft made-up songs with my mates and life didn't seem so bad after all.

Older people were kinder than younger ones, on the whole. I'd zimmer around Sainsbury's with Mum and elderly people would tell me to keep on truckin', relating stories about friends of theirs who had been in similar situations. Before Wil and I split up he had taken me to the seaside at Cromer for a few days for a change of scene, pushing me up and down the hills in my wheelchair. As he pushed me through town, an elderly couple came towards us, the man pushing his wife in a wheelchair too. They nodded and smiled at us, acknowledging us without making any judgment or any assumptions about me. It's funny; I wouldn't have noticed them before getting ill.

When something major happens to you, it changes your perspective on the world. You notice things that before would have passed you by. I see a lot of older people soldiering on now. Getting on with life, enjoying the tiny things, a passing smile, a bit of sunshine – treasuring what they've got without always wishing they had more. That is something I have learned to do as much as I can now. I try to live in the moment, without fretting about what I have or haven't done, or what I might do in the future. Just experiencing life moment by moment.

Lots of acquaintances became friends. Mum took me

to get my hair cut and my hairdressers were very kind, making little jokes and cuddling me. I had never been a super-cuddly person but hugs felt much more important now, a way of fending off the loneliness and sense of vulnerability I felt. It was mad; I don't think there was a moment after I left hospital when I was on my own, but I still felt lonely. I think I felt very out of touch with my body and myself. Looking back, I suppose it was simply depression. I went into a big sea of it. I had built up such a lovely life for myself and now it was as if I had gone down the big snake at the end of the Snakes and Ladders board. Back to square one. I had to be looked after like a baby. Everyone was concerned and worried about me and there was nothing I could do about it. My circumstances were forcing me to turn into a new person, and I didn't yet know who that person would be. I didn't know who I was any more.

I would sit on the swings in the local playground for an hour at a time. That might sound daft, but swinging was like being driven around in the car – you get the feeling that you are moving, that you are free, and you can forget for a while that you aren't. I craved the sensation of moving effortlessly through the air without having to think or to worry all the time about what my body was doing and what it couldn't do. I wanted to just be.

I had good days and bad days. There were days when I couldn't walk at all because I felt so weak, and those were so frustrating. The trick was to stop myself getting disheartened, to remember that there would be setbacks, that I would have bad days as well as good ones, and that was OK. Mum kept me on track, reminding me of all the things I had achieved, and reassuring me that despite setbacks I was making long-term progress.

However tough it got, I had to keep trying. Strangers often say things like 'Aren't you brave?' or 'I wouldn't be able to do it' or 'You're so strong'. I am none and all of those things. Everybody could do it. You would get through it too. You have to; what would you do if you didn't? You have to keep putting one foot in front of the other, even if it's the zimmer frame holding you up and not your legs. Fake it till you make it, bab! Even if you're moving backwards sometimes, at least you're moving. And you have to keep moving, otherwise it starts to feel as if it's never going to get better.

Slowly, my brain relearned how to talk to my leg. I fell over a lot, but learned to land on my right side as it hurt less due to the lack of feeling there anyway. You have to look for the silver lining in every cloud! I think part of the reason I didn't learn to walk sooner was the amount that was riding on it. So much depended on me learning to walk again and going back to my old life. The pressure I put on myself was a mental block. I'm sure I would have been able to walk sooner if I hadn't panicked about it. When I slowed down I realised I could do it, and when

I stopped being so proud about using the zimmer frame and realised it didn't matter, I started to improve.

When I first walked towards my mum without assistance and without falling I think she was the happiest I've ever seen her. Apparently when I learned to walk as a baby I just crawled backwards for a day and then the next day I got up and walked perfectly. I was nine months old and a properly ballsy baby. It sounds as if I had less trouble the first time round. I don't have kids yet and can't imagine what seeing me unable to walk again must have been like for my mum. There can't be many parents who have seen their kids learn to walk twice.

Mum has faced so much in her life, she's had so much to deal with, but her calmness and cheerfulness throughout is an inspiration to me. I am amazed that she manages to keep going, that she never gives up, but it is something I try to emulate. She has been an absolute rock. Whenever I ask her how she manages to keep strong, she says 'You just do.' In a very loud voice! I guess I've learned my way of coping from her: you keep going because there isn't any alternative.

Unfortunately, it wasn't just walking: I had to learn to write again too. I'd been putting it off for a while out of fear, but I had to tackle it. I was able to use my laptop to communicate, but I had to be able to use pencil and paper too. It wasn't that I couldn't remember how to write, it was that my right hand couldn't grip the pen properly. I still couldn't hold a cup without dropping it. I couldn't feel things fully so would grip them too loosely. The more I thought about it, the worse it got and the more upset I'd get. It was a vicious circle. The doctors reassured me that the sensation would come back in time but 'in time' wasn't soon enough. So I had to try to help myself. I didn't have anything to lose.

I spent ages thinking about the problem, looking for a solution. The main difficulty was that the sensation in my right side was significantly less than in my left side. If I put a pen in my left hand I couldn't write properly but I knew the weight of the pen, the size of the pen and my hand gripped the pen accordingly. But on my right side I couldn't feel properly so I couldn't get the grip right and the pen would fall. We all learn this as tiny children: watch a one-year-old for any length of time and you'll see that they spend a lot of their time figuring out what their bodies can do. We get out of the habit of learning new physical skills as adults. The only new physical skill most adults learn is driving, and I'd never had the money for that. So I was going right back to pre-primary school.

What I did was borrow a trick I had learned from something my mum told me about my brother. Jake is dyspraxic, which means his brain has trouble telling his body what to do. He has problems with movement and co-ordination, and used to bump into the furniture and drop things a lot. For most people, once we've learned to write as children, our brains automatically know how to write and concentrate, but Jake would have to make a special effort to tell his brain that he wanted to write. What I was experiencing wasn't the same condition at all, but Jake's symptoms weren't a million miles away from some of mine, so it gave me an idea. Following Mum's and Jake's instructions I learned to focus more on what I *saw*, not what I *felt*. I could see the pen, I knew what to do with the pen, so I would tell myself to grip it, experimenting until I gripped it tightly enough, and ignoring how it felt in my hand because those signals were wrong, they were deceiving me. Instead, I focused on how it looked and I practised, first with my left hand then with my right, until I got the grip right. Then I started to write. I thought that if I could teach my left hand to write first then maybe I could do the same with my right. And it worked!

The whole process took about six weeks. I still got it wrong sometimes, and the sensation I felt in my right hand varied – some days it was less, others more. But I would practise again and again, getting it right for each particular day. I never let myself think that I was going backwards, never allowed myself to worry about the long term. I just had to do the very best I could manage that day.

My first note said 'Today I started writing again, I could not be happier.' It's true. I couldn't have been. The only downside was I didn't get a gold star from my teacher, a special pen or my name on the blackboard. I guess just learning to write was enough!

The silver lining of all that effort I put into teaching myself to write with my left hand first was that I was now able to paint all my nails properly. I had learned to use my left hand with precision! I know that sounds silly, but before getting ill I could never paint the nails on my right hand with my left without getting half the bottle on my hands. Now I was Queen Ambidextrous I could do the nails on both hands for the first time. Small victories!

❦

With encephalitis there is often a stage when people get much better only to relapse, with different, sometimes worse symptoms, especially if they overdo it and try to rush their recovery. This is what happened to me after the first phase of illness.

Even though I had regained mobility, I still had the worst headaches, like no headache I'd ever had before – not with flu, not with a hangover, never. For ten seconds at a time it felt as if someone was pushing both sides of my head really hard. And then it would stop. But the mood I was in, nothing was going to hold me back. The minute I could walk the length of our living room I decided I was going back to work the following week. I thought I was capable of anything. Then Mum asked how my head was, and it was like a brick. When I tilted it back I felt as if I was going upside-down on a rollercoaster and my vision was like looking down a kaleidoscope at times. My short-term memory wasn't great and my concentration span nearly non-existent.

People kept telling me not to rush things, not to run before I could walk. But it was like when I was little and had just learned to whistle – I wanted to do it over and over again just in case I forgot how. I was scared my brain would forget how to do things again.

I found it very frustrating that I couldn't plan for anything. I still can't, really. I make exciting plans for what I'll do next week then frequently have to cancel them because my body has other ideas. I was trying to be normal but all too often that became a vicious circle. I'd do too much then get very ill again. I made a lot of trips to A&E. Often overnight stays, waiting there till 5am being tested for all sorts. Usually I was just sent home with some stronger painkillers and a follow-up appointment with a doctor.

The doctors thought the TIA, or mini-stroke, brought on by the encephalitis was causing the severe migraines and paralysis. And the only thing to do was to rest and not work. Which was tough: I'm rubbish at sitting still. Everything had changed since I got ill and I desperately wanted it all to get back to normal as quickly as possible. Everyone was keen to tell me what I could and couldn't do, but of course when someone says you can't do something, that's exactly what you want to do. So I started to build a mask to hide how poorly I was. I had previously had to hide hurt with bulimia so it wasn't hard for me.

In February 2012 I decided this was it, I needed to go back to work. It probably wasn't one of my best ideas but sometimes you have to try. Even though I felt awful I would go to my jobs in the Levi's shop and the pub, come home and sleep then repeat. I remember splashing my face with water over and over in the glass-washing sink at the pub on one shift because I'd passed out and didn't want to be sent home. Home was where I was allowed to fall apart and I couldn't deal with it.

I soon realised that what I'd done was about to bite me massively in the arse. By the weekend I was wiped out, and woke up with the worst headache I'd had since first going into hospital. The pressure in my head was insane and made me vomit. Mum took me to the doctor's and they put me in a quiet room. I lay down on the floor, which was about the only thing I could manage. A receptionist walked in and panicked, but there wasn't much anyone could do. Within two weeks of going back to work I ended up in hospital again. Exhausted and defeated, I spoke to my managers and I left my jobs.

I was locked in a battle with my own body. I found being with large groups of people very hard. If there were a lot of people in the house I would start to panic. I didn't want anyone to see me like this. I only felt comfortable in front of Mum and Jake and a very few friends. Though I badly needed company I hated it when all but a few trusted people came round. I would pretend to be asleep so I didn't have to have the same conversation over and over again:

'How are you?'

'Rubbish.'

'It'll get better.'

'Mm.'

So I would close my eyes and pretend I wasn't there.

Out shopping with Mum I would be OK for a while and then have to go back to the car. Which was ridiculous because I like people, I like company. But crowds, concentration and memory were all a struggle.

The strange thing was that I couldn't actually point to where the pain was. I could point to my head, but where exactly in my head I didn't know, and nor did the doctors. Months went by, and I had quite long stays in hospital for tests, where every ward round would bring another scary possibility or suggested treatment. One morning the talk was that I might have multiple sclerosis. Another time a doctor suggested I might need brain surgery. I was trapped on a rollercoaster of different diagnoses. It was terrifying, exhausting, confusing. As well as being in pain most of the time I had no idea what was going to happen, how long it would be before I got better – in fact, whether I would ever get better. Worse still, none of the doctors seemed to know either. The brain scans showed nothing, which in a way was great because it meant nothing life-threatening was going on. But it also meant that there was nothing to be fixed: you can't treat something you can't identify. One neurologist thought the headaches might never go away, that I would just have to have pain management forever: painkillers and acupuncture – maybe even Botox. Hey, at least I wouldn't get wrinkly! And I'd be sent home with another huge bag of painkillers and the promise of another appointment. Back to square one.

I'm strong enough now to admit that I spent a lot of time crying. I hate feeling sorry for myself and was too proud to cry much in front of other people, but long-term illness is traumatic and draining. Sometimes I even thought about calling the operator, just to have a cry to someone else, because I had heard that they have to listen to you for a few minutes before they put the phone down. I didn't want to talk to someone, I didn't want advice – I just wanted to tell someone I was falling apart and not feel guilty about it. It wasn't that I was on my own – I was surrounded by family and friends, but I still felt lonely, still needed to talk about what had happened to me and to cry over and over again. I didn't know anyone who had been through an experience like mine so no-one I knew was able to understand.

I kept my 'everything's fine' mask on with friends because I was terrified that they would desert me. I would try to look on the bright side, make plans to meet up, and then I would crash and cancel at the last minute. As a result, many friends came to see me as unreliable. They couldn't understand why I would cancel when I had been out with them just the week before. I'd become the flaky friend, all because I wasn't willing to tell them how bad things had become and eventually a few had had enough. I couldn't answer the phone, I couldn't meet for a coffee – I was just too poorly. It became easier not to fight for friendships, even though that meant I wound up still more isolated. I did, however, try to fight for one.

One of the loneliest places is arguing with a best friend. No, one of the loneliest places is probably in the middle of the Sahara with your last sip of Sprite and a moody camel. But at that time, the loneliest place in the world was sitting opposite one of my best friends and trying to fight for a friendship I knew was on its knees. The blame was shared. I didn't tell her enough and she wasn't there enough. I could handle a lot of people fading into the background – that was easier. Fewer people to disappoint. But with her I needed to have my say. So in a crowded bar, dosed up to the eyeballs with painkillers, I sat and waited. She came and we spoke and I raised my voice, which I never do – before then I can't remember raising my voice in adult life except when drunk. But when it came to it I just couldn't tell her how much I was struggling, how much I needed her and how I just couldn't take the mask off. At that point, not even for her. We bumped into each other a few times after, exchanged some catch-up texts and went our separate ways. It crushed me for a really long time.

Some friends stuck around, friends who had understood – friendships that had deepened over watching rubbish TV, hospital visits and understanding that being able to hang out wasn't something I could plan. Those moments had to be caught quickly because as soon as I was feeling good, feeling poorly wasn't far off. The good friends had nothing in common that you could pinpoint – they were all different ages, men and women, from all walks of life. But the keepers, the ones who stuck it out, have hearts of gold.

❧

When you're ill with flu, chickenpox or a broken leg, you expect to get better in quite a predictable way over a period of days, weeks, whatever. A doctor will tell you what is going to happen, roughly how long it will take, and usually that's the way it turns out. But it doesn't always happen that way with encephalitis, and it didn't with me. When I got out of hospital after the tick bite the doctors had warned me that the 'encephalitis headache' might go on for over a year. But I had no idea how bad this headache would be.

The feeling in my leg and arm had come back, but I was developing new, distressing symptoms. Some mornings I'd wake up and not be able to see at all for the first ten minutes. The hearing in my right ear kept going, as if I was underwater. I would sit at Mum's house, not wanting to be on my own, but unable to cope with the chaos there. Her house is like Birmingham New Street Station, wonderful and ridiculous at the same time, with three dogs, my brother and his friends, and his annoying habit of talking to people on speakerphone rather than actually holding the phone to his ear. I wanted to be a part of that everyday chaos. I had to keep reminding myself that I was still alive with everything to live for. I thought a lot about those wonderful women on the hospital ward when I first got ill – Margaret in particular, who had cared for me so brilliantly. About a month after I was discharged I got texts from Margaret's husband and daughter telling me that she had died. They said she had thought very highly of me and had been rooting for me to get better. I was very sad at the news.

I might not have made it either, and knew I was a lucky girl to have survived. But I would have given anything to go back to my old life of 60-hour working weeks and 4am finishes. The bit about long-term illness that isn't explained to you in the discharge lounge at the hospital is the sense of loss you feel: loss of your life before the illness, and all the trivial insignificant things you did every day without even noticing that you were doing them, and now struggle to do at all. I felt so lonely. I was drained by it all; I didn't know if I had the energy to rebuild myself again.

Sometimes I rebelled, determined not to let it affect my everyday life. One time I went out to a gig with my girlfriends, with orange squash and the occasional lemonade to spice up the evening. Everything was ace until the taxi ride home, but by the time I got into the house I had lost all sense of balance and felt as though I was going to throw up.

My head hurt all the time. It ached from the moment I woke up, like a smack on the back of the head. I would be blind for the first ten to fifteen minutes, unsteady for the first hour and then on and off again throughout the day. I was taking a crazy number of painkillers and other tablets, but nothing seemed to help. Any quick movement would make me want to throw up, as would too much noise. I found it very difficult to concentrate, losing words and forgetting what had just been said in conversation. I had never realised that listening to someone talk uses energy. I'd often forget most of a conversation halfway through. I bruised a lot for no obvious reason. It felt as if I had an imaginary friend who'd come and beat me up in the night. I was exhausted most days and spent four or five days a week in bed due to the pain. The noise at the supermarket checkout was almost unbearable – the beep-beep-beep of barcodes being scanned left me close to passing out. Car horns, sirens, the bass from speakers, yelling, looking out of the window in the car, bus or train, could all make me black out or feel faint and nauseous.

When I had the energy I would go to see my friends up at the Hare and Hounds for a cup of tea but it was hard because I felt I had no good news to tell them. I'd put on my make-up and shimmy in. When asked if I was getting better I'd say yes I was. Was I actually? No. But I didn't want to be a concern. I didn't want to be the bearer of bad news.

But underneath I was bored of being ill. Some days I wanted to take all the tablets in my bedside drawer just to get a good night's sleep – or to get away from it all. On those days I had to find reasons to carry on. Whatever the reason was, even if it was only going up the road for a cup of tea, then so be it, because otherwise I was fighting a losing battle between a headache and a drawer full of prescription medicine.

Chapter six

Everybody at some point in their lives will stand on the kerb and think "it would be so easy"

To Queen Treacs, princess among cats,
You have been an absolute babe throughout all this,
enough for me to forgive the time you didn't quite make
it to your litter tray and used my bed instead. It is about
time I told you something. It's going to explain a lot for
you. For example, the 'Grammys incident' where you
couldn't bear a second of it and sat with your back to
the screen throughout, even when Ed Sheeran and Elton
John were on, who you normally love. How it took a
while for you to get used to your glittery jewelled collar.
How sometimes you find yourself humping things and then
run off in shame because ladies aren't supposed to hump.
Well, Treacle. It was a sunny day back in 2009 when I
first saw you. You were handed to me in a box by an
elderly lady wearing an apron covered with flour. She
spoke very little English. I asked if you were a boy or
a girl; she said 'girl', and I left with you in my arms.
That is when our adventure began. Two young, free,
single super-babes ready to take the world by storm. I
settled on the name Treacle when I realised 'Mary J.

Blige' was a bit too much of a mouthful. 'Mary J. Blige! Mary J. Blige! Dinner time!' No. Treacle it was. You came everywhere with me. You loved bags, which made it incredibly easy to take you on the bus, in a taxi, to the supermarket. It was a nice way for you to see the world before you were ready to roam in it. You became braver and braver; each time the door opened you wanted to sneak through it. So that's when I took you to the vet to have your lady operation. So that you could have adventures without being harassed by cheeky boys. When I came to collect you, the vet told me you had been a brave boy. I corrected the vet, saying you were not a boy. He then showed me your boy bits. It's true, Treacle. You were born a boy. However, you had been brought up until that point as a little girl. We went home, and as I thought too much change would be taxing after all you had been through with the operation, I decided to change nothing. You had already acquired a sassy strut and a love of being preened whenever there was a chance. You were on track to becoming the ultimate Diva. The Beyoncé of the cat world. I didn't want to rain on your furry parade.

Whenever I have poorly days you come and sit on my pillow, or my head if that looks more comfy to you at the time. I often wake up to find you purring on my chest. Some doubters say that this is because you want

to be fed, but I believe it is because I am your
favourite person.
You've been amazing, Queen Treacs. Thanks for being so
lovely. If I could give you one million Dreamies (the
cheese flavour) I would.
Jodi
X

This is going to sound mad. It even sounds mad in my
head as I write it down. It only sounds mad in my head
because while I've been ill my days have been filled with
daytime TV and one-off shows such as the one where
the woman married the Berlin Wall or the bizarre one
where people dressed up as animals and went into the
woods to get frisky. Watch enough of those and you'll
definitely feel a bit peculiar.

Now, don't get me wrong – I'm not saying I would
marry my cat. However, she is one of my favourite things
in the world. They say (whoever 'they' are) that cats and
dogs recognise when you are ill or sad and I genuinely
believe this theory. Queen Treacs has been by my side
throughout the whole of this poorly period. Even when
I dressed her up as a pumpkin for Halloween she didn't
object for at least ten minutes, which is most excellent
for Treacle. She has a definite sense of style and refuses
to be made to look a fool. So, ten minutes was her way
of saying 'OK, laugh, you deserve it.' Again, at Christmas,

when I dressed her up as an elf, she gave me at least ten minutes before she made it clear that this was not to happen ever again. Treacs is very tolerant of my behaviour. And that is a part of why I love her, and a part of why I think pets are such a great distraction when we are feeling poorly. They don't judge, they put up with very odd behaviour, and they are just so lovely to cuddle and stroke.

I don't think Treacs can claim all the credit, but after nearly a year of hospital visits and tests and medicines I began to feel a bit better. Not well, but not as bad as I had been. I was trying to get back to normal again, so my friend Sarah and I decided to go to a local pub quiz for a quiet night out. The pub was only down the road from Mum's so I could get home easily if I started to feel poorly. As soon as I walked in I saw a man working behind the bar. He was hidden under a ball of hair and was wearing a shirt that swamped him. He wasn't attractive in a loud way, but had a warm smile and the kindest eyes. I noted this but didn't notice – not properly. He wasn't the kind of guy I had gone for in the past, and I wasn't really on the lookout for a new man.

Sarah and I busied ourselves with playing – well, cheating at – the pub quiz. The man behind the bar had a warm demeanour and it was as if I needed to know him. He looked as if he had stories, and I love stories. I asked another of the bar staff, a girl I knew, what his name was and she told me it was Sam. I always liked the name Sam. Later, she came over and told me that Sam had asked who I was too. Throughout the night we were like kids in a playground stealing glances.

I've always been pretty daring when it comes to making the first move. People mistake this for confidence but I put it down to low self-esteem. When you've had a low opinion of yourself for a long time any rejection from another person is nothing in comparison to your own rejection of yourself. So I walked purposefully up to the bar, smiled at Sam and demanded he take my number and text me the second he finished work. Sam was so startled that he spilt loads of Jack Daniel's all over the bar. Thankfully, he did text me!

Sam and I hung out the next day. He took me to the flat he shared with Foote, a loud, lovable Scottish guy. Their walls were plastered with pictures of jazz legends, their floors were strewn with beer cans and musical scores. Both guys were musicians. Sam had studied jazz at Birmingham Conservatoire and had left with a first-class degree. He played the trumpet in lots of bands and was passionate about what he did. With my love of music, nurtured by my mum and my grandparents from a very young age, I felt a real connection with this shaggy-haired boy – so we hung out more and more.

Sam introduced me to jazz and more experimental music, and in turn I taught him about UK hip-hop, grime and 90s R&B. Our common ground was singer/song-writers; we loved anybody who had a guitar and was spilling their heart out. We traded music and stories over and over.

From the moment we met, Sam and I clicked. We could be apart, but we just had more fun when we were together. Neither of us wanted a relationship at first as we had both come out of big relationships quite recently and didn't want to rush into anything on the rebound. Any more than a little something was off limits. However, the more time we spent together, the less easy this was to stick to. We fell in love.

Sam is an amazing cook. But I have learned that with his wonderful food comes a wonderful mess. He has earned the nickname 'Whirlwind Sam' as it looks like a natural disaster has hit the kitchen after every meal he makes. It's definitely worth the clean-up operation though. Another thing with Sam – he is one of those people who can pick up just about any skill. If he wanted to learn Spanish, he'd be able to – just like that. He's driven and passionate about what he wants out of life. He has worked hard to be as good as he is at playing the trumpet and knows that it is hard work that has got him there. He doesn't take it for granted and is always eager to learn more about whatever he can.

It was difficult telling Sam about my condition and all that had happened to me but I didn't have a choice. It took a bit of getting used to for Sam too. Mum and I had built up a way of coping with the challenges my brain throws at me, and a certain kind of gallows humour about it all. But Sam was straight in at the deep end. In his favour was the fact that Sam hadn't known me before so the dynamic of our relationship didn't change, as it had with Wil. When I told Sam about the encephalitis his first impulse was to try to fix it. Everyone does the same. I think it's a basic human desire: we want to do all we can to make something better. Sam was the ultimate ball of positive energy, constantly saying that it would get better. Mum and I had been living with the condition for a year and had become quite downtrodden by it, so at times we found Sam's relentless positivity annoying.

I pushed Sam away at first, just as I had with Wil. I wasn't ready to drag someone else through this. I tried to switch myself off when he was around, to see him less. My mum saw straight away what I was doing, and talked to us both about it. Sam reassured me time and time again that he wasn't going anywhere, that I could try to get rid of him all I liked but he wasn't going. I would have understood completely if he had. And if this relationship was going to turn out the same way as the one I'd had with Wil I felt I could really do without the heartbreak. But Sam was amazing. Anything that was thrown at me, he took on.

I found it hard to handle his optimistic attitude towards

my illness at times. I had stopped hoping I would get better and here was a new person full of hope – but I didn't want to buy into it. I had been hoping for a full recovery for months and I still wasn't better. Sam was being positive out of his own fear. The girl he wanted to be with was broken and he didn't know what to do about it. If he wasn't super-positive he would crumble. It took Sam three to four months to accept that he couldn't fix it, that he just had to be pragmatic. I didn't want to leave him disappointed, clinging onto something that might not happen.

In July 2012, soon after Sam and I met, our relationship faced a massive test. Following a change in medication I started having fits up to twenty times a day. I would lash out at people, hitting, punching and kicking. The fits were extremely violent, during which I had superhuman strength that I have never had before or since. I've never, ever been a violent person so this was incredibly weird and scary for everyone. Sam and Sarah, whom I was spending most of my time with, would try to pin me down to stop me hurting myself but I would have them up against the wall by my arms and legs.

For a while, if Sam was away, I shared a bed with Mum in case I had a seizure in the middle of the night. It would take Mum, Ian and Jake to control me. Ian is epileptic so Mum had a drill with him she could use with me too. When he was little, Ian's mum would know he was coming out of a fit if she said 'Twinkle twinkle' to Ian and he replied 'little star', as in the nursery rhyme. So that became our touchstone too. Mum would say 'Twinkle twinkle' to me, and when the seizure subsided I would say 'little star'. I was getting sicker and sicker, and had many sleepless nights to-ing and fro-ing to the hospital. Although I was aware that my body was misbehaving, I couldn't stop it. I hardly got any sleep at night and was exhausted.

I had a lot more tests in hospital. We were all frightened because the doctors didn't know why I was having these awful violent fits, and some of the theories they came up with were scarier than the fits themselves. The diagnoses came thick and fast. One doctor even suggested I would have to have brain surgery, with an incision straight across my forehead. He said it in a matter-of-fact way, as if it was simple and fine, drawing a line across his forehead as he spoke to show where the cut would be. It wasn't fine at all. I remember sitting down with some of my then-closest friends and explaining I might have to have brain surgery. But thankfully that was ruled out by the tests. I had loads of scans looking for bleeds on the brain. I genuinely thought I was going crazy. One moment a doctor would say something that clearly suggested I was going to die, then the next they thought it was just migraines or 'low mood'.

I don't want to be critical, because there are so many amazing, compassionate, wonderful doctors and nurses working in this country, but I have felt that my medical history has counted against me throughout my illness. The fact that I used to be bulimic meant that sometimes doctors didn't take my physical symptoms seriously, or assumed they were all in the mind. Not that it would be any less important if they had come from my mind, but I worried that straightforward physical causes might be missed.

There have only been a few situations when the doctors needed a real shake. Following a night of severe fitting, I woke up on the ward at my local hospital. I felt very sick. I had been shaking all over the place for the previous 24 hours so a little bit of nausea was a given. When I was brought lunch, the nurse forgot to give me an anti-sickness tablet, so I ended up being sick. The nurse then alerted the doctor, who said, whilst my door was ajar, 'Don't worry, she's bulimic. She has made herself sick.' I rang Mum in tears and she came straight to the hospital to discharge me. I wasn't up for an argument – I never really am – but if I saw that doctor again I would tell him off. Not only because he got it so, so wrong but because I'm not bulimic. I was once, and I suffered and fought to get over it, but that was five years before. If he had only looked at my notes and paid a little more attention, he would have seen that I was just very poorly.

After a month of me having fits, the doctors decided they were 'non-epileptic seizures', which meant they had no idea why they were happening but they were not due to epilepsy. Which in turn meant there wasn't anything anyone could do about them. Mum was at her wits' end and when we got home that day she decided to read all the leaflets that came with the medication I was taking. I had been prescribed a lot of different tablets. Mum noticed that possible side effects of a drug I had recently started taking included seizures and they also didn't sit so well with some other medication I was already taking. At this, she went properly nuts! I stopped taking those tablets and after four months of seizures, they stopped almost immediately.

♥

With the seizures over, we all had a bit of space to breathe again. But the crazy and wonderful thing about life is that it has a momentum of its own. It doesn't stop; things keep happening. People are born, get married, have families – even in the middle of chaos and uncertainty, and even if it feels as if you are stuck. Sam and I moved in together in October 2012. It was the house I had previously lived in with my friend Sarah, who had moved into the Jewellery Quarter of Birmingham. Sam and I slowly worked to put our mark on it, painting walls, making collages, making frames and placing little trinkets from our childhoods in every nook and cranny. It all started to feel a bit like home.

We got two more cats, Scootini and Tallullah, whom my first cat, Treacle, slowly came to love. She acts like their mum, although she is still unaware of why she has the urge to hump them from time to time. We blame the TV she watches, not the fact that she is really a boy. It wasn't even a year since I had broken up with Wil, and little more than a year since I fell ill, but so much had changed. Working, poetry, going out, all felt like a lifetime ago.

We had just spent Christmas with Sam's family and had come back to Birmingham to see mine. My mum dropped us home, and Sam asked me to go and make a cup of tea. My favourite thing in the world is lemon tea. And as I went to get some out of the cupboard, I saw a tiny box in there. In that tiny box was a tiny ring, which my best friends had helped Sam choose. An exquisitely beautiful, vintage diamond ring. I walked into the living room and Sam was down on one knee. He asked me to marry him and I said yes. He was shaking and I was so happy. It was such a lovely thing to happen and although we had only been together for six months it just seemed right. It was exciting, lovely, and something to look forward to. We had had a few sideways conversations as if we would get married one day, but I had no idea Sam was going to propose when he did.

We started planning for the wedding straight away. It would be the following year, in the early summer, and it would be perfect. We had no money at all, so everything would be home-made, which I love anyway. I decided that we wouldn't have fresh flowers: one, because they die and two, because I thought it would be lovely for the guests to be able to take a few home-made ones home with them. They would all be made from fabric that I'd got from the Rag Market in town. Flowers made from sequins, tartan, gingham, lace – I loved the idea of it being a DIY wedding. We started collecting things to put in trinket bags as favours: old cracker toys and pots of bubble solution. We booked a venue, an old village hall with massive beams across the ceiling in the middle of the countryside. It was beautiful.

But while Sam was the happiest boy, I began to worry and fret more and more. The fears ate away at me. I was engaged. I should have been happy, really happy, but I wasn't. I just didn't have the energy to enjoy it, to celebrate. I was still in pain the whole time, spending up to four days a week in bed to cope. And I felt guilty and upset because I wasn't able to be as happy as I wanted to be, planning the home-made wedding I'd always dreamed of, so I felt worse and worse. It was a vicious circle. Part of me was grateful for having survived, for being alive when I might have died, and for being able to live some sort of life. But for another part of me that wasn't enough – I was still grieving for the person I used to be before the tick bite. I hated feeling sorry for myself, but was angry about feeling poorly when I should have been in the prime of my life.

I didn't feel able to talk to anyone about it for a while – I felt too guilty that I wasn't happier. And so I began to take a turn for the worse. I started to have fits again, and this time the fits were stress-related. If someone shouted, if I spilt something or my head was particularly bad, I would fit. I was exhausted.

By February 2013 everyone could see that being ill was having a massive impact on my state of mind. I was becoming increasingly depressed; I was on antidepressant medication but it didn't seem to be doing much for me. I felt isolated and scared and in a limbo of a life I didn't feel I was able to truly live. My life was waiting for me – right there, with Sam – but I didn't feel able to live it. I had been unwell, up and down but basically not right, for eighteen months and I felt as if I was coming to the end of the road. The pain in my head was so bad that it sometimes made me suicidal.

I went to see a psychotherapist and spent ages crying, relieved to have someone who wasn't Mum or Sam agreeing that yes, it was rubbish, but that it would get better. Sometimes you need someone to come out and say 'Man, this is a pile of shit you're having to deal with, isn't it?' rather than giving you sympathetic looks or – worse – sitting awkwardly in silence. Sometimes you need someone to say what you already know. To give you permission to feel sad about what has happened to you, to stop you beating yourself up for not feeling better.

The psychotherapist asked what the illness made me feel like day to day. It's lonely but I'm never alone, I said. I feel as if I'm in limbo. I can't get on and do the things I should be able to, the things I really want to do. I'm a young woman; I should be out working, having fun, seeing my friends, planning my wedding and maybe thinking about having a family some time soon. I can't do any of those things, I told him. I've lost friends by not being reliable about keeping in contact. When I push on and do things it means I'm in bed for a week afterwards. I had never hated my bed so much, but couldn't remember the last time I felt fully awake. Some days I would spend all my waking hours looking at Facebook and Twitter, seeing what my friends were up to and beating myself up that I wasn't doing things too. I felt that life was passing me by.

I had always been busy, so busy. I'd been working all the time and because the people I worked with had become close friends it was one big social whirl. I thrived on the early starts and the late nights. It was hard being around work friends now because it was difficult to watch people living the life I desperately wanted back. I would have given absolutely anything to be able to work a twelve-hour bar shift again. The same people I had thought would be friends forever had become strangers who no longer understood what was happening. Or just didn't have time for it. Certain friends said things like 'I'm tired of knocking on your door and you not answering.' My answer to those people in hindsight? Text me. If I don't answer, ring me. If I still don't answer, go home and message me. If I still don't answer? Come back the next day and do it all over again. Because you cannot, ever, give up on a friend who is close to giving up on themselves. The real friends are the ones who never give up. The ones who know just how close you are to the edge and hold onto your ankles whilst you kick and scream and beg them to let you go. Those friends are for keeps.

♥

Everybody at some point has stood on the kerb of a busy road, or too close to the edge of the platform as a train is pulling in. Everyone at some point in their lives will stand there and think 'It would be so easy'. So easy to take one step forwards and then everything would stop. No more carrying the burden, no more worry or fear.

As someone who has spent time on that kerb I know that sometimes we don't need to be saved. Sometimes we just need a reminder that stepping away from the kerb is as easy as stepping forward. Because we've all been there, even the strong ones.

It was a grey February day and I felt as though I had nothing to look forward to. Sam had gone to a gig at a bar in town before I'd got in and I felt very alone. After yet another doctor's appointment without any answers I came home to an empty house. I was in so much pain with my head and was sick of not seeing a finishing line, not seeing a way out of this. I was sick of dragging people I loved through perpetual bad news. I scrolled through the contacts list on my phone and realised that nobody at that point could do anything to change my mind. I must have had phone numbers for 200 people, but none of them had the answer to what I was feeling.

I lay down on my bedroom floor. At that moment the floor felt like the safest place I could be. I was in a proper foetal position, going inside myself. I counted out my collection of prescription medicine.

I had over 300 tablets.

I was thinking about all the people who were supposed to be my friends and how right then I didn't feel like calling any of them. I didn't think any one of them could help. I hadn't spoken to any of them for ages. I felt I had been forgotten because the world had carried on turning without me. I tried to stop myself, but I felt jealous because everyone else was still living the life I'd had – going to work, the pub, hanging out, going to festivals – and then suddenly it was all taken away. All those people had gone on with it. I felt I couldn't relate to them any more.

Sometimes we get so wrapped up in our own bubbles that we don't see others are floundering and need help.

You don't see anyone write 'I really need someone' on Facebook. It's all good news. I couldn't go on Facebook or Twitter and say 'I'm probably going to kill myself in a bit. I really need someone to come round.' I felt there wasn't room for me in their lives, because I didn't have anything to offer them in return. Friends would ask what I had done at the weekend and I had nothing to say. I hadn't done anything. I felt useless. I felt that I had no worth and didn't want to be part of the world any more.

I felt completely numb. Even the thought of Mum wasn't strong enough to hold me back. I was gripped by an irrational logic, finding excuses for what I wanted to do. She'll be upset, I thought, but in the long run there will be less stress for her if I'm gone. It's fine, I told myself; Mum will be able to focus on Jake and life won't be so bad for her. If I'm not here, Sam will be able to find someone else who isn't poorly and they can live a better life together. If I never see my friends again then they won't keep asking me if I'm OK, and I won't have to keep saying that no, I'm still ill, and it won't be disappointing. All these thoughts seem ridiculous now, but at the time they were gospel.

I probably lay curled up on the floor for an hour, looking at the tablets, thinking of reasons to justify what I wanted to do. There were bright yellow and orange tablets, green and red. I had ibuprofen, paracetamol, codeine, diazepam, anticonvulsants, antidepressants, sleeping pills, tablets to counteract the side effects of all the other tablets. I was on 21 tablets a day.

I thought about who would get the cats. Sam was 26 and wouldn't want three constant furry reminders of me after I was gone. I thought about my mum and came to the conclusion that she would understand eventually but would probably never forgive me. I thought about my brother and my stepdad explaining to people what had happened. Would they worry they hadn't done enough? I would hate that.

Suddenly my phone flashed. I had downloaded an app called 'Princess Makeover' in which you get cartoon girls ready for their night out. It's a bit like dressing up Disney Princesses. I know, I am probably a bit too old for this. A message flashed up: 'Hurry up! We need our facials, big night!' This was so silly that I laughed at myself, and somehow that broke the loop. There was no other response than to laugh. Here I was, going through turmoil, thinking very seriously about killing myself, and the thing that saved my life, the intervention, was a silly app I'd downloaded that is aimed at little kids. Laughing at myself reminded me that I *could* laugh at myself, and if I could laugh at myself then the world hadn't crumbled just yet.

That second of distraction gave me enough time to understand that I could either sit there, letting my feelings consume me and potentially kill me, or I had to do something magical. It seems extreme to say that this group of animated ladies saved me but it highlighted that I wasn't ready to leave quite yet.

So what magical thing could I do? I had to be able to do something useful, something good. I wanted to use my time on earth well. All I had was me, a lot of free time and my love of writing. I hadn't been able to write poetry for a while and I certainly couldn't perform it because my memory wasn't good enough to remember it off by heart. But I loved writing, and I loved receiving letters in the post. I remembered the little notes that I had always left for people: on my mum's fridge door, in school textbooks, for waitresses, on the back of bus tickets left on the bus seat for the next person to find. What if these notes didn't get lost? What if they always found their way to the people that needed them? What if they were letters?

I put the tablets away. Within half an hour I had logged on to my laptop and set up onemillionlovelyletters.com. My aim: if I end up taking one person down from the kerb, then that's a success. That will be worth it, and I will have used my time on this planet well. I would do it through letters. In the UK alone, there are 62 million, 641 thousand people. In the whole wide world there are 7 billion, 38 million, 44 thousand and 478 strangers. And counting. And every single one of those strangers will have days when they need a boost. I started with a million, because that's a pretty big number – in fact the biggest number I could conceive of when I was a little kid – and being from Birmingham I use the word 'lovely' a lot.

So I sent a call out to every other person on the planet: if you, or someone you know, needs to be reminded how amazing you are, I will send you a letter. Anyone who needs a little lift, anyone who needs cheering up, reassurance or just a reminder that they are pretty lovely.

Thanks to Princess Makeover I was back from the kerb. I had inspiration, I had a plan, and I was all set to change the world, one letter at a time.

Chapter seven
Everything started to make sense

My website began with an 'about me' page and a message to anyone who might stumble across it. The message said:

> If you would like a letter, email me at
> onemillionlovelyletters@gmail.com
> Please include your address and why you would like
> one, for example:
> 'I'm feeling a little glum.'
> Wherever you are, whatever is wrong I will send you
> a little hug in an envelope.
> Thank you.
> Jodi
> xx

Within one hour of the website going online and sending a call out via social media I had received 50 emails from all over the world. The incredible thing was that the very first email came all the way from Australia. Imagine that! One moment you're on your own at home, lying on your bedroom floor and thinking about giving up, and the next you're talking to someone on the other side of the world. Amazing!

The first email read:

Hello,
I feel like I need a hug as my heart has been broken. I've lost my best friend and my foundation has been ripped away. Along with a totally shot nervous system I feel lonely and full of pain.
Hugs to you.
Phoebe

I quickly wrote an email back:

Hi lovely girl, send me your address and I'll get to it. It'll be with you this week. I'll make this hug a massive one.
Thank you.
Jodi x

The reply came:

Thank you so much! Thing is I live in Australia! I don't expect you to spend the money to send a letter here. I consider your reply and boundless generosity and kindness a huge hug and comfort in itself.

You're really making a difference, thank you sweet girl!

Phoebe xx

I can send one to Australia :) you sound like you need it! Jodi X

Amazing! I really do! Like I've never before! Beautiful. I'll treasure it always.

Thank you so much!!! Phoebe xx

So I got out my coloured pens and paper, glitter, stickers, tissue, string and glue (I've never been one to do things by halves), and sat down to write Phoebe a lovely letter. I wanted it to be perfect. This is what I wrote:

To Phoebe,

I'm sorry you feel so rubbish and poorly. Any stress you have on top of that is one hundred percent worse because you barely have the energy to deal with feeling poorly let alone anything else that is thrown at you. You said you lost your best friend. Any loss is rubbish and the pain it leaves you with some days feels like it won't ever stop. Maybe it won't, but it will become bearable, I promise. As for feeling low - try and remember what you were worried about this time six months ago. I bet you can't, right? Worry fades. It does get better. As for being lonely - you are a beautiful girl and have a lot to give to the world. Go out there and grab it by the balls! Be your own hype - don't focus on the bits that aren't great, lovely. Instead, concentrate on making today a better one, even if that's just by going for a walk. I know that sounds clichéd but you have to grant yourself those tiny victories some days. You don't have to move mountains every day - start with a small pebble.

You are magical: Start believing it, missy!

I hope today is wonderful.

Lots of love,

Jodi

xx

Hearing from Phoebe was a wonderful breath of fresh air. Even though she was hurting, I knew she would be OK, and the fact that she had reached out brought me such comfort. It took me right back to being five years old, writing a letter to my nanny in Heaven.

Phoebe may have lived on the other side of the world but I could totally relate to her experience. She was alone a lot of the time too, she was lonely and she too had lost her best friend. I know what it is like to lose friends for reasons beyond your control. And I know what Phoebe meant about having a shot nervous system, because I have been poorly and am a worrier by nature.

What I tried to say to Phoebe is that things really do get better. Life moves on, worries fade. Of course we'll always have problems of some sort – that's part of life – but I truly believe that as we learn from experience, worries come to seem less significant. We can cope with whatever life throws at us because people are built to survive. The real killer is worry. If we can teach ourselves to stop worrying, we'll be able to cope with anything else just fine.

And guess what? Phoebe wrote back to me. I got a card in the post from Australia:

Hey there, Lovely,

Just wanted to write to say that I received your lovely letter the other week! Thank you so much – your words and thoughts are inspiring and reminded me that I must stay grateful for the good things in life. I can't tell you how nice it was to get your letter in the mail – all the way from the UK – I will treasure it always. A big warm hug that I really needed! I am so appreciative! I've been meaning to write to say thank you and tell you that you have made a real difference with me and you're such a lovely soul.

Lots of love. Keep smiling, beautiful girl, and thank you once again – I'll never forget it!!

Phoebe xx

Phoebe cheered me up more than I could ever have imagined. Writing to her made me feel as if I had a purpose again, that my life was worth something. The moment I began writing I felt happier; everything started to make sense again. I had been in the darkest place, and writing to Phoebe and people like her got me through that time. It was truly wonderful to be able to focus on others and not keep going round and round in circles about how lonely I was feeling. Now I had reasons to get up and face the day. I couldn't just leave these people; they needed my help.

One of the next emails I received was about a woman who lived in Oman. This was exciting – I'd never heard of Oman before, let alone been able to communicate with someone from there. Suddenly it was as though the whole world was in my inbox. I felt lucky.

To Jodi,

I have actually lived in Oman (a little-known country in the Middle East) for almost my whole life. It is lovely and there are lots of good things about being here but it's like living on an island. There are only so many people (not all of whom are entirely right in the head, it could be the heat?), limited places to go, limited activities and gossip is rife! Luckily for me a friend of mine from school days has also moved to work here. She is amazing and without her I would

probably have gone mad and moved into a shack in the desert to raise camels. Unfortunately she is really down at the minute. A guy she was seeing has treated her really badly and she's been left with a broken heart. She's also going through a world of work problems at the moment and could just do with a bit of love. All of this came out in the last week! Not really the best. She's not hiding under her duvet and ignoring the world which is pretty good going and I'm doing all I can to remind her that she is loved and that things WILL get better. I thought that maybe a little unexpected love and kindness from the other side of the world might make her day/week/ month. I fully understand that you're probably super busy sending kindness around the country and post here is about as slow as in the middle ages. Though I do hope you don't use carrier pigeons! We use postal boxes rather than getting letters through the door. We don't really have street or house numbers it is more 'the house with the dome on the corner by the palm tree where the red car parks near the Intercon hotel', a bit tricky for the posties. If you could find time to drop her a little line or two that would be wonderful! Love,
Aneeka

So I wrote to Anneka's friend, Cath, in Oman:

To Cath,

This is just a little note to remind you how wonderful you are. You make the world a lovelier place and you are so loved. You are so kind and supportive of others. I'm here to tell you that sometimes when we feel like our worlds are upside down is when we really start thinking what's best for us.

Those brick walls are there for a reason - they are there to give us a chance to show how much we want something, how much drive we have to make our lives magical. They aren't there to stop those who are like you. Those people who want to make something wonderful with their worlds. See the setbacks as boulders to stand on to scale those walls, Cath. You are super special and you are going to leave such a wonderful mark on this big world. Believe in yourself - everyone else believes in you. You are beautiful and strong. These grey clouds will pass.

Find your sunshine, sweetpea.

Jodi xx

The story in the next email was so close to my experience it took my breath away.

Hi Jodi,

I am also 24 and I'm feeling a bit sad. I was diagnosed with MS this year. I was trying to look on the positive side but I really wasn't feeling very well. However, in the last couple of weeks I have completely recovered (I lost the function of my entire right side) and somehow this has made me less positive. The joy when my toes began to move, the elation when I could pick up a drink with my right hand again is all gone – now I am faced with the fear of waiting for another relapse.

I strongly believe a positive mental attitude is half of the battle in any situation – you are living proof. I have lost my way on the positive path a little, and I am sure a letter from such an inspirational girl will spur me on.

Best wishes,

Sarah xx

To Sarah,

Congratulations, lovely girl! You should be so happy. You may well relapse at some point but this isn't something to fear. What I do is make lists: a list of things to do when you're feeling good and a list of things to do when you're feeling rubbish. On the bad list, write down all the box sets you want to watch, all the films you've planned to see but never did and the books that have been on your shelf collecting dust - read them. Rest up. Do not fear these days, Sarah. I know it's rubbish not being able to do much/anything but you have to give yourself a break. Stick two fingers up at your bad days, Sarah - you are in control of them. You deserve every last bit of happiness, sweet pea.

Enjoy every good day, rest on the bad ones.

Big love,

Jodi

xx

Jodi,

You are in the process of making a million new friendships by doing one million lovely little things. 678 so far, Twitter tells me.

Thank you for my pick-me-up; I hope this acts as your one for today.

Stay strong, happy and healthy.

All my love and respect,

Sarah

xxx

Sarah is ace and we chat on Twitter quite a bit. She is my age and we have a lot in common, so can easily relate to one another. Even though we don't have the same medical condition the effect is the same: we both spend a lot of time not being able to do much. So I tried to give Sarah good advice about resting and staying positive. If you're having a bad day there is no point beating yourself up by dwelling on the things you can't do, which will only make you feel worse.

Our world is frantic. Everyone is in a rush – busy busy all the time. In practically every other letter I write I have to tell people to take some time for themselves, to value themselves more. And the more I write it, the more I begin to follow my own advice. Don't compare your life to other people's; focus on the things you can do; be kind to yourself; give yourself permission to rest and relax; enjoy the little things. I'm so free with dishing out advice but need to learn how to follow it myself! That's the amazing thing about writing the letters – even if I'm feeling down myself I can still write to other people, and after writing a couple of letters I usually feel better too.

Sarah emailed me again recently to let me know how she is getting on:

Hey Jodi,
I'm doing much better – I've managed to pull myself out of the black hole. I have just finished my phased return to work, so I am back to 40 hours of desk sitting. Yawn. But it is good really as it means that my

legs and arms are working again – yay! There is no
lasting damage (apart from some brain scarring, but
we'll gloss over that bit!) and I am on daily injections,
which should help to control the MS. I've enrolled
myself on a 'getting to grips' course at my local MS
Society Centre; really taking the bull by the horns.
Information is power – that's how I'm tackling it all.
Let me know if there is any way I can help with the
project.
I really do believe that what you are doing is
helping people – there is nothing better than a
smile spreading across your face when you're
feeling blue. I hope the universe returns its dues to
you one day.
Take care, sweets.
Sarah x

Sarah didn't know it, but the universe was already
returning its dues to me. The more letters I wrote, the
happier I felt. It was like when I hugged my head teacher,
Ms Penman, all those years before.

Paying it forward made me feel good inside.

I get lots of emails from people writing on behalf of
someone else, like this one. I guess they're paying it
forward too:

Hi Jodi,

I think what you are doing is awesome, and I really hope that life deals you a good hand soon and your illness improves. You deserve it :-)

I'd love if you could write my girlfriend Penny a letter. She's 23 and has struggled since university to find a job that she's passionate about. After over a year of job hunting, she had to settle for something that she's never really enjoyed for financial reasons and I think she worries that she'll never be able to get out of it. I know, and I've told her, that when the time comes she'll find something she loves and I'm certain she'll be great at it, but sometimes that's not enough.

From,

Dan

X

To Penny,

This is a little note for you on the days you don't think it's going to get better to reassure you that it will. You make the world a lovelier place, Penny, and on behalf of the whole world I'd like to say thank you! This job is just a means to an end - see it as that. This is just a job to help you pay the bills whilst looking for your dream job - and it will come, Penny, I promise. The job you are in now is not the job you'll be in forever. You write your

story – nobody else. And yours is going to be the
loveliest story, sweet pea.
Everything will turn out wonderfully. Keep your head up,
sweetheart.
Lots of love,
Jodi
xx

Penny wrote back to me too. It was brilliant – all of a
sudden I had a brand-new collection of pen pals.

To Jodi,
Thank you! I bought this card over a year ago because
I fell in love with its message: 'Believe in people.' Since
then it has sat in my drawer as I felt it was waiting
for the perfect recipient. Then I received your letter!
You are doing wonderful things, Jodi! You helped me to
remember to BELIEVE IN PEOPLE. Keep at it, my lovely.
We need people like you. Here's to loveliness, good (or at
least better) health and success. THANK YOU, JODI.
Lots of love,
Penny from London (who WILL find a better job)

Having to do a job you hate in order to pay the bills
can be a little soul-destroying, but you have to keep telling
yourself that it isn't forever. At one point I was doing three

jobs at the same time. There was one in the bead shop, Beadasaurus, which I really liked but it didn't pay the bills so I had to get two other jobs that I hated every second of. The absolute pits was being a waitress in a strip club. Thankfully I didn't have to stay very long, but only because I got more shifts at my third job, which was in a pub. Now this job was the lesser of two evils. I didn't have to wear sequinned hot pants but I did have to deal with violent drunks and being leered at by much older men. I was doing enough shifts there to quit my job in the bead shop. It kept me sane while I was doing the other two but it didn't pay enough. Mad, I know, but if you're struggling, you do what you have to do to make ends meet.

Before too long I left all those places, good and bad, and worked in the Levi's shop and a nice pub, the Hare and Hounds, so it all worked out fine eventually. I know it will for Penny too.

Hi Jodi,
My name is Kate. I'm going through a pretty rough time in my life right now. I've lost all my confidence and when I'm not at work I'm in bed. I feel like I've failed in life and most days I don't even want to be alive.
I think I need a letter to feel like I'm worth something :-(
Kate xx

Hi Kate,

This letter is a reminder of just how lovely you are. The fact you are going to work even on your bad days is a small victory - you need to grant yourself the tiny things that you get done. They count - you count. You are allowed to be sad and cry sometimes because life isn't all sunshine and rainbows but on our darkest days you need to remember that there are still rainbows out there, there is still sunshine. It's good to make yourself get out of bed and walk outside - not even out the front because sometimes on these days we don't want to see people. Make yourself a cuppa, go and stand on your back doorstep and tell yourself that you are incredible because I already think you are - it's you that you have to convince. Not even convince - just remind yourself. I have so much faith in you, Kate. You haven't 'failed in life'; these days life begins whenever you want it to, and you have so much left to do. Don't be scared - if your dreams don't scare you they aren't big enough. You are capable of anything - remember that on the days you feel like nothing. It's going to get so much better, I promise.

I hope today you are smiling.

Lots of love,

Jodi

xx

I got a lovely hand-written letter back from Kate too.

Hi Jodi,

Sorry that it has taken me so long to reply to your lovely letter. This feels like the hardest letter I have ever had to write but I wanted to thank you for taking time out of your day to write to a complete stranger in the hopes of cheering them up. It worked. A lot has changed since your letter. I have left my unhappy relationship and moved back home with my parents. I am already a happier person and this is all down to you and your letter. You have saved me. I think what you are doing is wonderful and it's amazing how the kindness of a stranger can have such a powerful effect on a person. Please accept these stamps as a small token of my thanks and to help you in your task of writing one million lovely letters.

Thank you again,

Love,

Kate

P.S. I read your letter every day and carry it with me always.

Kate's first letter is very short, but if you read it slowly and think about it you'll see how terrible she is feeling. Saying you don't want to be alive is a serious call for help. It isn't something you just throw into conversation, and Kate's words really shocked me. What I wrote to Kate is what I would want my best friend to say to me in the same situation. It felt like my responsibility to make Kate feel that it would be all right, that she would get through this, and that there are some things she can do to make it a bit better. Just little things, like going outside every day. Above all, I wanted to tell her that she matters. I really wanted to get that message through to her because so often we forget that everybody matters. All of us.

I could totally relate to Kate. But the next email was beyond anything I have experienced.

Hello, my name is Olivia, I'm fifteen and live in Brighton with my mum and two younger brothers. We moved to Brighton from Scotland about three years ago due to domestic abuse. After two and a half years of suffering alone and living with a man that would one minute be a loving stepfather and the next minute my worst nightmare, I came home and found police everywhere, a smashed-up house and Mum lying on the floor crying, covered in cuts and such a swollen face she could hardly speak. Most of the close friends we told didn't believe what we were saying, despite the bruises and cuts – they couldn't get their head around a man they saw as nice, caring and funny doing such horrible things. It was hard for us to get our head round it too, so we understood them not being able to accept what we were saying.

On my fourth birthday, my dad left me. I never thought about my dad's side of the family, until two weeks ago when I had a message on Facebook from a woman I hadn't spoken to since I was eighteen months old telling me a man named Daniel had died, and she'd spoken to my dad about it and that the funeral was on the 18th of February.

It was only when I asked mum who Daniel was and saw her face drop that I realised he was my granddad. Last week I was registered as a young carer for my younger brother, Tom. He's ten, eleven in April, and autistic, dyspraxic and epileptic. Mum doesn't deal with him very well, even though she works with vulnerable and disadvantaged people. I always think it's because dealing with other people's problems are easier than dealing with your own. Whenever I say this to her she denies it, but I know she knows it's the truth.

I'm the only person who really gets him, and takes the time to understand his problems and find solutions and explanations for them through the only ways he understands – art and science. It gets hard sometimes – he has certain ways of doing things. My other younger brother Ollie, has major anxiety

problems, in some ways worse than Tom does. He's
really protective over Mum, so much so he refuses to
sleep in his own bed and so sleeps in hers, and won't
go to sleep until she's in bed. We all know it's
because he's worried something'll happen to her, but
he won't admit it. He's literally the most stubborn
nine-year-old to ever inhabit Earth.

Ollie tries his best, bless him – usually too much.
He's always trying to help around the house, but a
lot of the time mum takes it as him getting up to
mischief, so now he's given up trying to be good
altogether. He just shouts at everyone, being aggres-
sive, going out of his way to irritate, and much more.
Like a normal nine-year-old, but times it by ten.

And then there's me; a fifteen-year-old in the middle
of her GCSEs. School is hard – even though I'm a
straight A student, or was. Stress at home has led to
severe migraines, so I miss quite a bit of school.

This is why I'm sending this to you. Sometimes it's
easier to talk to strangers about your problems
because they get to know the real you. You explain
your life from the start and tell the truth because
you don't have to keep contact with them if it turns
out you don't fit together as friends. You've got
nothing to worry about, to hang onto – just the fact
that they're a stranger who doesn't know you, which
means you can help them and they can help you.

That's what I find anyway.

Simply writing this essay of an email to you has made it a lot better. Just sharing my story with a stranger has helped.

Thank you for being you.

Olivia x

To Olivia,

You have no idea how strong you are - your kind heart makes you powerful beyond measure. You are so brave and have such a mature head on your shoulders; you've had to deal with more than anyone should. That doesn't make you a victim, Olivia. You are a survivor - you, your mum and brothers.

My dad has never been around. What I've learnt is that this is not a reflection on us but on him; your dad is weak and it's his loss, Olivia, because he has missed out on an amazing daughter! Tell your school about being a young carer because if you are ill during exams you may get special consideration, which will make you less stressed. Your brother Ollie is trying to be the man of the house, which is completely understandable. Why don't you three get out of the house for an afternoon? Whether it be just going to the park, just something to remind you both that although you have been through some pretty extreme circumstances you are still allowed to have fun, you deserve it. Maybe, suggest to your mum that she gets counselling with the NHS. There are charities supporting young victims of domestic abuse too, so consider contacting one.

You are all going to be just fine, sweetheart. You are a beautiful girl, Olivia. You are intelligent and caring and you have the brightest future ahead of you. None of this is your fault. Stay positive, strong girl.

Love Jodi xx

When I knew I was going to be writing this book I got in touch with some of the people I had written to, asking if I could include their letters and stories. I wanted to take extra care to check with Olivia because she is so young. This was her reply:

Hello!

I have heard, yes, and I'm so, so excited about it.

I would totally love to be in your book! Can't even describe how happy this has made me!

I'll type the letter up for you now. I would scan it but yesterday I was on my laptop whilst drinking tea, and my right hand shook (it shakes now and again, I can't control it), and, well, RIP laptop.

I'm doing OK, thanks! I can't go to school at all right now; they think I'm having mini-strokes, which is a bit of a bummer. School has been great, though, and they're sorting me out a home tutor for

September, so hopefully that'll stop me from falling behind on all my work.

I'm starting up a new project where I go to public places, and ask strangers to write something about their favourite person or something that's happened to them that they'd like to write down on paper, or just something beautiful that they'd like to share. I'll then display them all in different ways – bunting, framed etc. Then there'll be a big exhibition of them, so all the community can come and view them.

There's a lot of bad things going on in my community right now, and I think everyone just needs to realise that there are beautiful and amazing people around us; it's just the media doesn't write stories about them and so it makes it seem like there's more bad people.

How are you doing?

I'M SO EXCITED FOR YOU. You're a massive inspiration.

Lots of love,

Olivia x

Olivia is only fifteen but she is wise beyond her years. She has had every ounce of rubbish thrown at her but seems amazingly strong about it all. I read her letters and wonder how she hasn't fallen apart, why she hasn't crumbled. I'm not sure I would have been able to cope with all that at her age. I see things in Olivia's experience that I can relate to, but her experience is more extreme than mine was. Perhaps Olivia is proof that deep down we are often stronger than we realise. I really want to keep in touch with her and am so pleased that when Olivia feels bad she writes to me.

Hi,

My name is Abbie. I saw your story in the paper and I have to say I admire what a selfless and beautiful thing you are doing! I can only hope to become like you. I am often guilty of getting wrapped up in my own woes too often! While I would love a letter for myself I would really like you to write to my mum. Four years ago my dad Patrick died of a heart attack. In the years before he died we lost all of our money and our home, and we moved into a small council flat as my dad was no longer able to work. When he died needless to say we were not left with much and we borrowed money from friends for his funeral. I am the youngest of five children. My mum really struggled after this: they were together for 40 years and she was the one who found him at home when he died. We have a big family but I feel in the last few years the family has drifted apart slightly and due to their own grief are not too supportive of Mum. My mum turned 60 last year. She works several jobs to pay the rent and would do anything for her family. However she often gets down at the outcome of her life, she just about manages to pay the rent and sometimes borrows money for bills. She doesn't ever see her life getting better. Last year things got too much for her and she tried to take her life. She has been to counselling since and is now in a good place. She is a lot happier and we are really close, although I can see she still gets down and is overwhelmed at what her life has become. I love my mum – she is amazing. She is beautiful and looks 40 instead of 60. She makes friends with everyone she meets – everyone immediately likes her and she isn't prejudiced towards anyone. Above all she is amazingly generous and will always put my needs before hers! Her name is Tanya. In many ways I feel guilty asking you to do this for me. I really hope your health improves and please believe me when I say how incredible this is of you! I can only dream of being as selfless!

Lots of love,

Abbie x

To Tanya,

This is just a little note to remind you on the days when you forget just how amazing you are. You make this big world a little bit more magical and you have so much left to do here! You are beautiful, people feel lucky to have you in their lives - you make so many people happy, Tanya! It's only right you should be your happiest too. You work so hard - please know that people massively appreciate all the hard work you do! Things are going to get better - you're in control, Tanya. Make a list of all the things you want to do, from small things like reading a certain book or big things like going to Peru. Give yourself a ten-year window and cross as much stuff off as you can. I'm sure Abbie will help you on your adventures - and you've got so many to have!

You are so loved, Tanya, and I really hope you have some lovelier days. You really do deserve it.

So much love,

Jodi

xx

When I wrote to Abbie asking if I could put the letters about her and her mum in the book, I received this amazing reply:

Hi Jodi,

We would love that! I will give you a little update as well. Since I wrote to you requesting a letter, my mum went into hospital and was diagnosed with ovarian cancer. She had a grapefruit-sized tumour on her ovary and was operated on four weeks ago. Your letter came two days after she had her operation and I took it into hospital with me as a surprise for her. She loved it and it was a fantastic pick-me-up and really helped her through it!

Today she went into hospital for a follow-up to her operation. The cancer was contained enough that the doctors removed it all in the operation! She will have three-monthly reviews but for now she is deemed cancer-free. Our worries about the devastating effect that the treatment and disease would have on our dear mummy have now disappeared and we are all thrilled! We really reflected on your letters in that dark couple of months of worry and we would like to say thank you so much for your kindness! I really hope you receive all the love, kindness and support that you deserve! We have realised that the world is a beautiful place and that life is to be cherished and it's due to acts of kindness like yours!

All the love in the world,

Abbie

Xxxx

Writing to Tanya felt like writing to my own mum. Like everybody, my mum gets down sometimes. It's easy to get stuck in a rut and start thinking that the only way is downhill, particularly when you're older and have taken a few knocks. What I said to Tanya is what I would say to my mum. I always want her to know that she is loved and has so much left to do.

Like Tanya, my mum is beautiful and kind. Just because their children have grown up it doesn't mean that mothers' lives are over. Now is the time to stop worrying and start enjoying yourself. Mums don't go on the scrap heap when their kids are grown.

Life isn't just for surviving, it is for living. If you've had too much rubbish thrown at you, too much to cope with, it is easy to get locked into a mindset where everything feels like a military exercise, but it doesn't need to be that way. If you have too many problems to deal with you can start to believe that you deserve it all, that this is just what your life is like. But life can change in an instant. Things change. It might be a tick bite that sets you off down a long, difficult path, but it might also be meeting a stranger in a pub who turns out to be the love of your life. It might be something wonderful. Life is for living and you have to go out there and grab it. Just because bad things have happened to you, it doesn't mean they always will, or that that is what you deserve. There's a big world out there and there is so much for you to do, at 30, 50, 70, 100. Tomorrow will be brighter.

Hello Jodi,
I'm a 32-year-old French Canadian guy so we don't share anything in common except the same queen.

I've recently come across your story and could not believe how unfair life can be sometimes. But what strikes me most is your ability to overcome adversity and challenges and to use them as positives.

I may not be in your situation but I have my own struggles. For years I've been fighting with dysthymia, a neurological problem that can basically be described as chronic depression. So, as you can imagine, motivation does not come easy for me. I've been mostly down the last few years and have struggled to keep a job, friends and, well . . . a life. Every time I read a story like yours it helps me push through a few more days, more weeks and maybe months. I've recently gone back to school to try and change my life and it has been incredibly hard to keep up. I'm again struggling with depression and lack of motivation, self-esteem and confidence.

It has been the plague all my life. So why would I need a letter from you? Because stories like yours are what drive me to continue, they are what motivate me to get up in the morning and face the day ahead of me. I need to be told, to be shown, that there is light at the end of the tunnel. People like you are that light. I need to learn how to wire my brain like yours. I need to find strength in adversity and motivation through failure.

I'm sure you get hundreds and thousands of

requests. I'm probably not the one in the worst
shape requesting a pick-me-up . . . but to me in my
little world it would make a huge difference.
Thank you for sharing a piece of yourself and your
kindness to the world.
Matt xx

To Matt,
You are incredible and strong. Getting through each day
with depression is a victory - you are winning the fight,
Matt. It's a tug-of-war and sometimes it may feel as if
depression has the upper hand but it never has control.
You have the other end of the rope and on the days
when you are feeling strong you can pull it straight into
the mud. You are stronger than you think - you are in
control, lovely. Each day remind yourself that you deserve
happiness and to get the most out of life. Depression is
not going to win, because you won't let it. You are so loved
and you are never alone in this fight. Your grey skies will
clear, there is sunshine beyond the storm, always. I promise.
Hope you have a lovely day, Matt.
Big love,
Jodi
xx

Although each battle with depression is different, I can
understand how Matt feels to an extent. I see it as a

tug-of-war between the rational side, which knows things will be OK, that bad feelings will pass, that there are millions of reasons to enjoy life, and the depressed side which says everything is rubbish, there are storm clouds overhead, it's all grey.

I'm not sure if everyone with depression experiences this tug-of-war but I do, and my battle is to keep the depressed side down. Some weeks the rational side is winning, others the depressed side pulls back, hard. The more you write down the positive things, talk about the positive side, count your blessings, the more the rational side of you suppresses the depressed side. If I could be out and about a lot I could be with other people, which is important for keeping the rational voice alive, but because of my condition I can't, I'm stuck at home a lot, so I have to do it myself by writing.

I think depression will be there, in the background, for me and for Matt throughout our lives and we have to find ways of managing it. The trick for me is to make the good bits as big and loud as possible, and always to remind myself of the lovely bits. And there are some really lovely bits.

We can all help each other by being someone else's good voice, someone else's louder voice. When someone we love is having a rough day, it's easy to send them a text or leave a note for them saying how wonderful they are. We don't listen to ourselves enough so we need other people to remind us how amazing we are.

Hi there,
I am a seventeen-year-old girl recovering from an
eating disorder and am looking after my mum who
has been diagnosed with depression. I would love a
letter to pick me up when I have a down day and
when I need a little smile. You are inspirational :)
Lots of love and best wishes always,
Grace x

To Grace,
You are the amazing one! Every day you are in recovery
is a reason to be proud of yourself. It's a long road but
you will get through it and your eating disorder will no
longer be an active part of your life. Never give up
because nothing will fill you with more joy than looking
back down that mountain you've climbed and thinking 'I've
made it!'
You are strong and right now you and your mum are
battling separate battles - which you will overcome
together. There is no greater team-mate than your
mumma! You are a beautiful girl, Grace, with a wonderful
future ahead of you. This is just a blip! It will get better,
so much better.
Lots of love,
Jodi xx

Grace is fantastic. She's more than halfway there. Now some say that if you have had an eating disorder it will always be with you, and I think there is a bit of truth in that. However, as someone who has had an eating disorder and has been through the recovery stage, when there is still the temptation to not eat, or to be sick, I think you get to a point when you can say that the eating disorder is a part of your past and not a part of who you are now. You can say that you *had* an eating disorder, not that you *have* an eating disorder. When I was in the grips of bulimia I thought that point would never come. I thought that I would be bulimic for the rest of my life. But I'm not – I have climbed the mountain and am on my merry way. I've been to the top of the mountain, looked back, and can say now that isn't who I am any more. And I'm confident that Grace will climb the mountain too.

When I write to people I often include information about support groups and charities that can help with their particular problems. There's one for eating disorders, especially in young people, called B-eat, which I have found helpful in the past. You'll find contact details for this and other groups I recommend at the end of the book.

Hi Jodi,
I'd love a hug in an envelope. More than you'd know!
I am struggling with my business. It's new and it's

hard work. I'm not scared of that, but I am scared of money troubles!

I'm having a hard time with a boy I like and a part-time job I had fell through so it's back to square one!

I know you'll be busy sending letters so don't worry if you don't get round to me. It's a lovely thing you're doing. And you should know that.

Lots of love & hugs,

Charlene

Hi Charlene,

Firstly I'd like to congratulate you on your new business! That's ace, you must be so proud and happy. Of course it's a bit scary! You're fulfilling a big dream, and if it wasn't scary it wouldn't be a big-enough dream. You're a talented, strong lady, Charlene - if you are determined enough it will all work out! Do not worry! Make yourself happy in your new little kingdom and if the boy is still acting up he doesn't deserve you. You are beautiful!

Jodi

xxx

Jodi,

I hope everyone had the idea to write back to you, because sometimes it's nice to get something back. Thanks so much for my letter. It was much needed.

Well . . . the best I can do is say a little prayer and
make lots of wishes for you and Tweet you pictures
of cute animals!
Keep smiling, you're AWESOME!
Lots of love,
Charlene xxx

Often when I'm writing these letters I'm not really
doing anything except reminding people of things they
already know but have lost sight of. It was easy to write
to Charlene because there were so many good things in
her letter. I just needed to remind her of what she already
knew. She was saying that she had a new business and it
was hard work, but she isn't scared about that bit so why
wasn't she congratulating herself? She'd told me about
the bits she should be proud of, but had just put everything in the wrong order! She has a new business, that's
amazing, and she's achieved it at a young age – that's
inspiring. Charlene has so much going for her and if this
boy doesn't appreciate her then he doesn't deserve to be
included in her big adventure. Sometimes we just need
people to tell us what we already know for it to sink in.

Hello there!
What a wonderful idea for a project. I imagine you've
already been inundated with requests but if you get
time I would love a letter. I've spent the weekend

feeling sorry for myself after pining after a boy (who, I hate to say, does not feel as enthusiastic about me as I do him). A million Kate Bush songs later and I still feel more miserable than Sad Sack from the Raggy Dolls. Good luck with your project. I think you're magic.
Charlie
:)

Hey Charlie!
You are a beautiful girl who doesn't realise her worth. This guy does not deserve an inch of you if he can't recognise just how lovely you are. And you are just lovely (start believing it, Missy!) so don't waste your love on someone like that. Delete his number. Now!
You need someone who will treasure you for the magic you are. He will come.
You're ace.
Lots of love,
Jodi
Xx

To the wonderful Jodi,
It was a while ago that you sent me my lovely letter. I didn't reply straight away but please don't think that it wasn't appreciated! It was very much so. Your kind words have brightened many days (every time I read the letter back it makes me smile).

THANK YOU :)
You're one of the most inspirational, magical people. Keep up your fantastic work. I guarantee you have no idea how much joy you bring to everyone you meet, write to or to anyone that listens to your poems on YouTube.
YOU'RE A STAR!
Lots of love and a massive THANK YOU again,
Love,
Charlie

P.S. Also enclosed: a little 'love' patch. Thought I would give you some back. (Feel free to pass it on again if you so wish) :)
And . . . a little homemade worry doll. Her name is Cariad (which is Welsh for love). She is a very good listener. She likes reggae music, powerful hand-driers, black and white movies and the odd glass of sherry.
xxx

Charlie is a sweetheart and really funny. Her letter and gifts really made my day. This is her most recent update:

Hi Jodi,
I'm afraid I still pined over my sexy tramp (I call him this because I think he is super-gorgeous but his hair is scruffy and he has a face that looks as

though it's dirty even though it's not). Well, one night around Easter I found myself in the same pub. There was a group of us. We all sat down (just as well as I was in full swoon mode) and ended up playing a game. We laughed lots, drank beer and everyone was perfectly merry. That night my sexy tramp and I hooked up. Hoorah!

However... he has now left the country to go and work abroad for five months and I very much doubt that anything will happen on his return. Despite still finding him very lovely and funny and cool, I have realised that I deserve more. I'm pretty sure that I am a fun person to be around and I try to be as kind and thoughtful as possible. Reading your letter gives me that confidence boost when I need it. He may well make me go weak at the knees but I feel much more centred and grounded now.

I am a huge fan of this project. Sometimes just knowing someone out there is listening takes away a lot of the heaviness.

I wish you all the luck in the world. You totally deserve it!

Lots of love,

Charlie x

I, along with many others, will be able to relate to Charlie's letter. I haven't always placed my heart in the hands of someone who knows how to look after it – or even wants it – and all it leads to is a very bruised little heart. So when I read letters like Charlie's I know what to write. I know what I needed to hear at the time – that you are worth more than somebody who doesn't appreciate you for who you are. Don't waste your time on people who don't want to spend time with you. That sounds like a real mum thing to say but it's true.

Hi Jodi,

My name is Sofie, I'm from Holland and I read your article in the newspaper today. What an amazing initiative! I really admire you for doing what you do while you are ill. Usually people who suffer from really bad headaches and dizziness need a cheer up! Well, I would be so honoured if I could receive a letter from you. I'll tell you why. My boyfriend and I just broke up, and all of a sudden I realise how lonely I am. I just moved out and now I'm all alone in this city with no friends and no soulmate. I know it sounds pathetic, but I'm sitting here in my apartment, alone. No parties, no love. I'm trying to make the best of it by playing guitar and enjoying the small things in life, but it's hard when you're sad. And it's still snowing here!

Once again, it's amazing what you're doing! And get well soon!!!

Regards, Sofie x

P.S. I would love to send you a letter back!

To Sofie,

You are <u>so</u> special! See this new chapter in your life as your next adventure. You say you feel alone – you are not. It's going to be hard adjusting to being on your own again but it's not a bad thing! You do have friends and people who love you. Your soulmate is still out there, Sofie – you haven't found him yet but he is and he'll be wonderful but in the meantime learn to love yourself and your own company because you are amazing! Go and have some fun, Sofie. You deserve it!

Lots of love,

Jodi

xx

Dear Jodi,

What a surprise that you've sent me a letter! All the way to the Netherlands! Thank you so much for your lovely letter. I still feel amazing and I'm so glad that I dared writing you an email. Your letter has a special

place in my room. Now I'm making you a postcard and I
hope you like it!
Greetings from the Netherlands...
Lots of love,
Sofie
Xxx

We don't always want to admit it but sometimes our
partners are our stability, our rock. So when you break up
you're bound to feel lonelier for a while, even if the relationship wasn't great because initially we tend to edit what we
remember from the relationship and focus on the best parts.
When they're gone you go through a period of feeling the
most alone you've ever felt in your life. I felt like that after
I split up with Wil. But it will get better for Sofie. Time
does heal, even though it doesn't feel like it at the time.

As the weeks and months passed I received and wrote
more and more letters and emails. Hundreds and hundreds
of them. It was magic. We have no idea what stories a
person has to tell, stories of strength and of love and of
hope that mostly go unknown because they are untold.

I was opening emails to find messages ranging from
the fourteen-year-old girl who had just started to self-
harm, to a group of women my age who had lost their
best friend to cancer. Stories of abuse, loneliness, grief,
self-doubt, exam stress, depression, long-term illness, lost

souls, heartbreak and people who just needed reminding that they matter, that they are enough.

Some people didn't need a letter, just a listening ear, while others needed reminding that not only were they amazing but the world simply wouldn't be the same without them.

Reading through all the letters it may sound like I have it all figured out. I definitely haven't. It's a lot easier giving people advice than taking it yourself, but through writing my letters and learning from various messes I have got myself into I have gained a little bit of understanding and wisdom that I hope may be able to help others.

What 'One Million Lovely Letters' has shown me is how similar we all are. We are often made to feel worlds apart. Some countries only seem to exist on our TV screens in the midst of disaster. But reading letters from two heartbroken girls who have lost their mums, one in Surrey and one in Ghana, they sound like exactly the same person. The only difference is the 3,167 miles between them. We are all connected through our experiences of grief and loss.

I've learned there is no pattern to the type of person who contacts me. It isn't a certain age group, or from a certain place. It isn't just people in the sticks who write to me, it's high-flying executives, surrounded by people all day, who want a bit of post from me because they need a little reassurance.

I've written to Betty, who is an absolute babe from Massachusetts. She is 86 and loves all things British. She sent me pictures of her garden and got her daughter Karen to write back to me as her eyesight isn't so great these days.

There's one-year-old Halo, who isn't allowed to open her letter until her eighteenth birthday. I told her all about the project and how her parents had wanted her to be the youngest participant so far. Until then it will be kept in her memory box by her lovely mum and dad.

I've learned that we are all too quick to judge sometimes. I often found myself looking at the avatars of people sending me the letter requests and thinking that he or she was too beautiful to be broken. I soon realised that the face tells you very little about what a person has been through.

I set up the website onemillionlovelyletters.com to help other people, but it has helped me too – more than I can begin to say. I have no doubt when I say that it saved my life. Hearing about other people's worries, other people's troubles, helps me to accept my rough times too. And it makes me feel I have a purpose again.

The more I hear that others are having a tough time, the less alone I feel. It sounds crazy but it's like creating a worldwide society for the lonely and the heartbroken. It's as if we're all sitting around in a big online community centre saying 'You know what? I feel rubbish too.' Telling other people that it is going to be all right is slowly but surely chipping away at me until I've come to believe myself that things will be OK. And if I have brought just one person down from the kerb, then that is a good use of my time on earth. That's why, even though it is a responsibility, writing the letters never feels like a burden. All people are asking for is a lift, and that's not hard to deliver – it's easy to make someone feel good. The only difficult thing is finding time to write enough letters – to be sure that everyone who asks for one, gets one. Also the upkeep of the One Million Lovely Letters desk can be troublesome as it frequently needs to be de-glittered, de-stickered and has a real knack for eating pen lids.

People ask me how I know what to say, but what I do doesn't involve a remarkable skill. The reason I can relate to people is because I have been on the kerb in so many ways – through long-term illness, suicidal thoughts, depression, eating disorders, bereavement. I've been there loads of times and I've come back. And I know it will be all right. Sometimes all you need to be reminded of is that you are loved and you are not alone.

Chapter eight
Life goes on...

24 September 2013

To Sam,

Tonight, after you left for the last time, I expected you to walk back in, tell me that this break-up was ridiculous and I was more than just an illness and this was worth fighting for. And I'd have let you in - tonight I would have let you cuddle me to sleep and worry about tomorrow in the morning. I don't care about tomorrow, not tonight. Put your hand in mine, just one last time, and let's pretend that love is enough. On its own, just love. No strength needed because tonight our love is carefree, no worries, no tablets, no nap times. Just us. Tonight I would let you be right, you could have your say over and over. Because tonight I am missing you over and over again. The bed feels massive. It's not even that big but tonight it feels like I could fit galaxies in it - like the galaxies between us. Tonight I've never felt so far from home. We text pleasantries because we don't know how to be without each other. The cliché 'We are two halves of a whole' always made me cringe but we were part of a whole, even though we had holes in. Today I cried seven times - not massive cries, just bits. The first when the lady at the café gave me free coconut and lime cake, the second when our neighbours brought me flowers. Three when I phoned the council tax department to notify them you'd left and the man said I sounded too lovely to leave. Four when a friend came to visit and that opened the floodgates because with certain people you know your tears are safe. Five because Treacle wouldn't come in when I called her and I ended up having a loud conversation with a cat who wasn't listening about how I was too sad for a fight tonight. Six when I boiled the kettle and went to use the cup my mum gave you featuring instructions on 'how to make a good brew'. You hadn't quite mastered it yet. Seven when the TV show *The Fried Chicken Shop* had an unnecessarily emotional twist. A couple more tears were thrown in as a bonus at the checkout line at Asda after they played Gabrielle's 'Out of Reach' and the Sugababes' 'Too Lost in You' back to back.

The next morning you text me to look for your passport. You said you would come and collect it around 12ish. So I got up, put on my heart hair clip and a little bit of mascara and lipstick because today I just wanted to make it a little harder for you to leave. Put on enough blusher to look alive, go downstairs so that by 12:05 I'm sat tea in hand, halfway through a TV programme so it doesn't look like I've been waiting by the door for you. You text 'Make it half two x'.

I go back upstairs, shower and start again.

There is something desperately sad about the idea of crying in the shower or in the rain. So I didn't cry, I just stayed sad. Every other minute I remind myself it is a physical impossibility for my heart to fall out, even when it feels like it will. You are stuck with that pain in your chest and your tummy and it will be OK. Apparently, hope so, one day, maybe, we'll see.

Tonight I started following adorable pics, cute emergencies and tiny animals all on Twitter. I'm currently searching for pugs dressed as pork chops to make all of this seem OK.

For now it just hurts though.

Jodi x

Sometimes we end up having to say, or in my case write, something we never thought we would. Sam and I broke up. Although we split up for the right reasons it didn't stop the first few days being excruciating. But this time I decided against sending late-night text messages or quietly crumbling. Instead I just wrote to him. A letter I would never send or share with anyone but needed to write. One of the many things I've learnt from the people

I have written to is that sometimes the process of just writing things down can make your heart feel a little lighter.

26 September 2013

To Sam,
Today I felt like I'd been kicked in the stomach, completely winded all day long. I kept trying to think of power ballads I could listen to that would reassure me things will be alright. I sat on the kitchen floor whilst Mum divided up the spice rack. When Mum asked whose the star anise was I pretended it was mine, though I don't even know what star anise is. I kept it for a few minutes because I could and then placed it in your box with three mugs and lots of bottles of balsamic vinegar. You own loads of it. It feels really silly to pack all of it but I don't use it and I don't want to be referred to as that spiteful girl who threw all of her ex-boyfriend's vinegar away just because she could.
You text to ask 'How is your day going, lovely?'
I wonder how to answer this for ages. Now it's night-time again and you are packed into six boxes, eight bags and four storage containers that are full to the brim with bits of you.
The next day I swapped the gas and electricity to my name. I'm sure they didn't want to know why I am now

a single occupant but I told them anyway. Ramanpreet from the gas company spoke to me so nicely and I told her to stop because I would cry and she told me not to because that would make her cry, and I reckon she would have, for her own reasons. She passed me over to a man named Jon and whilst transferring me described me as a sweet lady and told me everything was going to be OK. I know it will be eventually, but she said it in such a lovely way it reassured me immediately. Jon said 'Out with the old and in with the new gas bill' and wished me luck. He said 'It's the first few days you have to keep your head up.' And I am, and I'm fine most of the time.

Tallulah brought in half a mouse earlier and I cried because it was dead and you would have got rid of it and it was just another reminder that you were no longer here.

Jodi x

28 September 2013

To Sam,

Today I didn't have to adjust the height of the shower head or the temperature. It was a goodbye kind of morning. I found the last bits of you around and placed them in their boxes. And I didn't cry. It's weird – all of this week this hurt has been something I couldn't recognise; it isn't the same as previous heartbreaks. I'm not the same person this time around.

My brother dislocated his shoulder once and had to have it re-set. And it really hurt for a little bit but then he was OK. If they had left it, he'd just have had a wonky shoulder and it would have hurt and restricted him from doing all sorts. I guess this is like that. I woke up and I wasn't sad, I wasn't angry because there is nothing to be angry at. Some fights can never be won, some hurt can't be taken back however angry you get. The loss associated with those moments, it all stays lost.

I've been heartbroken before but this feels like we've saved each other from walking around with a wonky shoulder and that realisation made me laugh, then smile. And I hoped wherever you were, you might be smiling too.

Love

Jodi x

Technically my heart should be in tiny pieces at this point, but it isn't. By the laws of Jodi, I should be an absolute mess. I should be texting my ex-fiancé saying how much I love him and that we should try to work things out. I should be scraping the last bit of cookie dough out of the ice-cream tub whilst wailing to Adele's album *21* – which, by the laws of Jodi, should be the anthem for this break-up as it was for the one before. I should be doing terribly.

However, I'm not. I'm actually fine. Not like when someone says 'I'm fine' but they're all misty-eyed, while their bottom lip shudders up and down (possibly to the rhythm of 'A total eclipse of the heart'), and rejects any sort of hug as it will be that bit of human interaction that sends them over the edge. I don't feel like that at all. Granted, initially I was a little bit wobbly but that was more down to the fact it dawned on me that I am now a single mother to four babies. Furry babies, but babies all the same.

What I have been feeling is guilt for not falling apart. I feel that after a year and a half, surely I owe it to our relationship to have some kind of mini-breakdown, for it to mean something in the grand scheme of things? But that hasn't happened; it's been bearable. And I think the reason it has been bearable is that for most of the past year I have had an inbox full of moments when people have needed to know it will be OK and I have told them that it will be because I truly believe it will. Whether it's a broken heart or a really bad week, one by one we've been fixing each other with our letters. I never expected the thank-you cards and the emails I receive from people I've written to but those little bits of kindness I get back let me know that this project is working, and that even on my dark days I will be OK too. So I guess you could say that it has been a worldwide effort to make sure that this time my heart stays intact.

It's totally clear to me now that we all have the same basic sadnesses – heartbreak, loss, illness, depression, bereavement. I don't know what it is like to live in a war-torn country, but I do know what it's like to have your heart broken, and that feeling is the same worldwide. When I broke up with Sam I saw how many strangers understood what I was feeling. So I've kept on writing my letters, and I've kept on believing in the kindness of strangers. And my lovely letters inbox helped heal my broken heart.

♥

Loads of people have wanted to join in the letter writing. Everyone who got in touch, right from the outset, connected with the idea that we can 'pay it forward', that we can be each other's positivity, each other's ray of sunshine. The idea appeals to people young and old. Betty and her daughter Karen, the women from Massachusetts, USA, even sent me a beautiful box full of coloured paper so I could write more letters. They really wanted to join in the letter-writing project themselves.

Others have invented ways of using letters that I'd never even thought of. Since being ill I've spent loads of time waiting in doctors' surgeries and that can make you really glum. So I thought this email was a brilliant idea.

Life goes on . . .

Hi there,

I saw your blog post – I wonder if you could write a letter for me to leave in the waiting room of the doctor's surgery I work at (but can you not mention in the letter that a member of staff requested it, in case I get into trouble)? We have a lot of elderly and vulnerable people, especially women, using our services, and I know some of them will get a real lift to read a friendly, upbeat letter, instead of all the donated issues of *Take a Break* and *Heat* magazines! Many of them are lonely and very unwell (physically and mentally) so I know they could do with hearing some positive, supportive words.

If you want to write more than one letter that would be amazing (I can replace the first one, as I'm sure whoever finds it will probably want to keep it!) but it's OK if you don't have the time!

Can you please send them to my home address?

Cath

Thanks so much! This is a beautiful project! :)

X

Doctors' surgeries are quite tense places to wait in. You don't really talk to anyone. People are there for such different reasons: one might just have a cold, while another might be waiting for the results of the scariest test of their life. I find the silence frightening. Sometimes you just want the person next to you to ask how you are. It's never fun waiting for results so I thought a nice little letter would be lovely.

Hello you!
Yes, you! This letter was requested for you by someone who works at the doctors' surgery, just to remind you how wonderful you are because sometimes we tend to forget. I know you are feeling poorly but hopefully this little note will make you smile, even if it is just for a second.
You need to rest up. It's not easy being as lovely as you are all the time! You are so loved and well thought of and on behalf of the whole world we cannot wait until you are back to 100%.
Hope you have a lovely day.
Love
Jodi

Jodi,
Thank you for the lovely letters! I enclose some stamps for future letters you want to send to others :)
Take care,
love,
Cath
X

Life goes on . . .

The emails kept on flooding in. They were a good distraction, keeping me company on the days when I was feeling blue. Sometimes there were so many more than I had expected I couldn't keep up with them. At one point I had over 700 emails requesting a letter in my inbox. Loads of people wanted letters for someone other than themselves. We're a generous bunch, on the whole!

Hi Jodi,
I'm Lee. I was wondering if I could get a letter, not for myself but for my girlfriend Meg.
She's eight months pregnant, baby's doing great but she isn't. She feels run-down and achy most days, unattractive even though I tell her daily I love her and think she's beautiful. She's just generally having a hard time with the whole pregnancy thing!
A letter from you would cheer her up a lot!
I think what you are doing is incredibly selfless and the world would be a much nicer place with more open-minded people like you.
Thanks again.
Lee

To Meg,
Congratulations! I hear you are going to be a mummy really soon. I hope your last month of pregnancy is lovely and quick! You are so beautiful, Meg, and you have a

boy who thinks you are the most delightful lady on the planet! And he's right! I know you are feeling rough at the moment but I promise this will pass, sweet pea! It's completely normal to feel worn out; you are carrying another human being around with you all the time. Although he/she is a super treasure, I can imagine he/she is also super-heavy and can make you really tired. You are on the home straight and you are going to be an amazing mum. You are so loved, Meg, and you three are going to make an amazing team.

I wish you and your team every happiness, wonderful girl. Lots of love,

Jodi x

A little while later, Meg posted this lovely comment on the website:

Hi Jodi,

A couple of months ago while I was ill in bed my boyfriend gave me a letter that had come for me in the post. I didn't know he had written and told you that we were expecting our first baby, and that I wasn't having an easy pregnancy and had been very ill and was struggling a lot with it. Reading your letter actually made me cry happy tears and I continued to carry it around with me during the rest

of my pregnancy. When I was ill just reading it cheered me up and still now when I'm worrying about how good a mother I am, and I'm doubting myself, I read it. What you do is amazing and I love how something as simple as your letters can change someone's day. Thank you so much for my letter. I have now placed it in my daughter's memory book so she can read it when she's older so she knows there are amazing people in this world just like you.
Meg

That kind of response makes me feel this project has to be worthwhile.

Dear Jodi,
Can you send a letter to my mum Karen? She has been feeling really down lately and she just needs to know that we appreciate her so so so (times infinity) much.
Ellie

To Karen
You are AMAZING. You make this big old world so much LOVELIER, just by being in it. You have done such a wonderful job with your daughters. They absolutely ADORE you! They are so happy and that is your doing - you are an INCREDIBLE mum. But now it's time for you. You

still have so much to do, Karen. Your husband thinks you are the BEES' KNEES, because you are! You think about the whole world before yourself. This is the whole world saying 'Focus on yourself, Karen'. You have the best co-pilot who wants to go on adventures with you. It's in your hands, lovely – do something every day for you.
Lots of love,
Jodi
xx

I really enjoy writing letters to mummies because it's like writing to my own mum. She is the best person in the world and I find it hard to express how much she means to me, so I love telling other mummies how amazing they are. It sounds like Ellie feels the same way about her mum too. And so did this lady.

To Jodi,
I don't think I particularly need or deserve one of your letters. I have to say I am extremely fortunate to have a very happy life, I have a wonderful husband and a beautiful daughter. Although as I write this I have started to think of things. The main thing that brings me joy in my life is the same thing that causes the most pain. My daughter Ella is 9 and if you remember, like I do, little girls aren't always that nice. The girls in her class recently have been

mean and nasty to her and even though she talks about it and doesn't seem all that bothered (we have bought her up to be a strong self-assured little girl) it really bothers me. This is my little girl, my baby! I want to protect her from the world, I want every day to be full of happiness and smiles. But life isn't like that and I seem to have more problem coming to terms with that than she does. I tell her that you're not a kid forever and when you grow up this won't happen, but we all know it still does. And I will until the day I die worry about her and how happy she is and feels. They don't tell you that when they talk about having babies!

Thank you so much Jodi.

Caroline

This letter really resonated with me because of how my own Mum must have felt when I was getting bullied at that age. I can always remember thinking my Mum was a superhero, she had this ability to just make me feel better however bad the day had been. I wanted Caroline to know that she would be Ella's superhero too.

To Caroline.

You sound like a really amazing Mum. Although you can't protect Emma from everything, having you by her side is as good as having the biggest army. You'll never realise

just how much she appreciates you - although you will want to go into her battles for her, picking up the debris, sewing her heart back together and dusting her off is a job I have no doubt even from your email you are going to be just amazing at. You will be her greatest ally, best friend and the best Mum. Do not beat yourself up Charlie. Keep doing what you are doing so well. She is so lucky to have a Mum like you.
Lots of Love,
Jodi

Hi Jodi,

So, um, here's why I'm not happy.

I've just come back from a two month trip to Sicily where I think I was the happiest I've ever been and now I'm back in wet, cold England and it doesn't feel like home any more. I miss the Italian language so much and the sun and the food and the people... It also sucks to be home because now all the friends that took a year off are all gone and I honestly have no friends left. The ones that took a year off are now travelling and the ones who go to university have now gone back. The idea of staying in this cold, wet country makes me so sad but it's unavoidable. To get out of here I'll need money, and to get money I'll have to work. Here. In England.

What you're doing sounds great and I'm glad people like you exist.

Beth xx

I am completely in favour of big adventures. I think people should have as many as they can for as long as they can and learn as much as possible about our big old world and the people within it. However, after seeing a new bit of the world coming home can often leave us feeling deflated. But the perfect time for adventuring is while we have few commitments – which is what I wanted to reiterate to Beth. Just because she has come home, doesn't mean she can't leave again. Whilst her friends are at university is the ideal time to go and gain knowledge and experience of new places and meet people from all over the world.

To Beth,
Go and find your bit of sky. Work here for a little bit, get through Christmas then start your New Year with a list of where you're going, because you can actually do that. Nobody in the world can stop you because you are not tied to anything and that is an amazing thing – you should be so excited. Make enough money to get some-where and get comfy – then work – and keep doing it for as long as you possibly can, as long as you want to. You will make friends all over the world, make stories and

laugh and do it for as long as it makes you happy. You deserve to be so happy! See this as a pit stop, recharge your batteries, refill your wallet and the world is yours. There is nothing more exciting than that.
Lots of love,
Jodi xx

To Jodi,

I think you are amazing. Someone wrote about what you do on Twitter and I can't believe I've only just discovered you, if purely for the fact that I write letters constantly. I write to people to cheer them up, or when I need cheering up. Sometimes I write to myself – okay, often I write to myself – to get my feelings written down and often I write to people to tell them how I feel about a situation, or why I'm mad, or what I've done. But I hardly ever send them, often because I am worried about how people will react if I tell them how I really feel.

And I keep every letter I'm written (there aren't many of them). I read them back when I need cheering up, which is pretty often recently. It's my final year of A levels and stress and anxiety and depression are getting on top of me. Next year I hope to go on to study at King's College London to become a doctor, but at the moment I just feel pretty down in the dumps. I need cheering up.

Aaaaand, there we go, I'm rambling. So yeah, just to let you know that I think what you do is magical and I would love love love to receive one of your lovely letters. The world needs more Jodi Ann Bickleys.

Love, Lucy xo

To Lucy,

This little note is to remind you that you matter. You really do. We often rule our troubles out as not important – but they are, lovely girl. You have so much to look forward to and your dreams are yours. Let the excitement of achieving them consume you – not your doubts. Put those doubts in the bin; they will do nothing for you! You are amazing, Lucy. Go and show the world your magic!

So much love,

Jodi

P.S. You will be an AMAZING doctor.

Writing a letter to yourself, as Lucy does, is a great way of working out what's bothering you. More often than not we know the answer to our problems ourselves, but we lose sight of it. By writing everything down we can bring the situation back into focus, and hopefully find the solution. Sometimes there isn't a solution, but it helps to get everything out of your system by writing it down anyway.

Dear Jodi,

I was going to write to request a lovely letter (I'm in love with a boy who's leaving for Colombia in about twelve hours' time and I'm not sure that's long enough for me to convince him to come back!)... Then I read your 'about me' on the website, which made my gloominess seem rather insignificant. I'm not that good at letters but I *love* sending postcards so if you would like me to send *you* a postcard then send me back your address and I will :)

Sian

Hi Sian,

Did you tell him? I hope he knows how much you love him — he'll be back! If it's a more permanent move then Columbia is an aeroplane away — so go and get your love. He's lucky to have you! Remember, missy, that you are worth coming back for! You are beautiful and kind. Never for a second think your problems aren't as important as anyone else's — especially mine. It's all relative. I've had this drummed into me before so I feel I am able to do the same for you. Love is worth all the rubbish little bits like this — it makes the lovely bits so, so much better.

Now, go out there, you pretty lady, and book your ticket

to Columbia (or at least email the boy). I hope you're having the loveliest day, sweet pea.
Jodi xx

Dear Jodi,
Many thanks for the loveliest of lovely letters. It's an amazing thing you're doing – it must feel nice to write all those lovely words knowing they will make someone smile. Good luck with the rest!
Love and thanks again,
Sian
xxx

Guess what happened next!

Hi Jodi,
I emailed you because my boyfriend had to go back to Colombia. Well... you were right!!! We have stayed in touch and he's coming back!! In July!! To work! Forever!! Well, not forever but... until his next idea. Your letter was so lovely and I really believe in your project. I think it's an amazing thing you do. Also I used to work as a psychologist with people with acquired brain injuries (which sounds like what you have?), so when you talk about your 'bad brain days' I do have a small understanding of what you mean.

Sending you love.
Thank you x10000000000000000,
Sian xxxxx

So things do work out! Not always, but often enough for us to stay optimistic.

❧

One of my favourite things so far was leading a Lovely Letters workshop with a class of eight- and nine-year-olds. Don't panic! I didn't talk to the children about grown-up problems, just told them that some grown-ups needed cheering up and that it was their job to do it. Working on the project with children was ace. I rested for a week in preparation and took a massive bag of glitter and pretty paper for the kids to use. The essence of One Million Lovely Letters really shone through in the children's letters. Being kind, for no other reason than to be kind, wasn't an effort in this classroom. These children didn't ask big questions, didn't need to know a lot about the people they were writing to. They just got on with writing a letter because all they wanted to do was make the person who received it smile, whoever they were and for whatever reason they needed it. So for two hours, with two different classes, that's exactly what we did: wrote letters to people who needed a smile, just because we could.

We began with Kirsty, who really needed cheering up:

Life goes on . . .

Hi Jodi,

My long-term boyfriend just unexpectedly left me.
After years together, a shared cat and a shared flat, he
just left. Worse than that, he didn't actually leave. He
broke up with me then stopped coming home while
he stayed in the bed of a girl I knew well. And then
he came home and told me he missed me, had sex
with me, before changing his mind again. It took him
two months of screaming at me every time I cried,
telling me to move on, before he actually moved out.
Now I'm living in a flat that's a broken shrine to my
lost relationship. I'm in a town that I hate and that I
came to for him and he's moved back to London. I
know no-one, and have too much anxiety to leave
my flat in case I bump into this girl. She's really
mean. She was sort of my friend, except she's five
years younger than me. Now when she sees me she
sneers. She told me that 'she won'. I can't take seeing
her. She reduces me to a child. I speak to no-one.
I've forgotten what it's like to be confident, and I've
forgotten the sound of my own voice. I've started
speaking to my cat as if she's my only friend because
right now, she feels like it.
I just want some contact from the outside world.
Thank you.
Kirsty

I wrote this to Kirsty:

To Kirsty,
You have no idea how beautiful and amazing you are.
You're not supposed to - leave that to those who love
you. They are the true proof you are doing something
right. That you are enough. Even the bits of you that
you dislike, they think are wonderful. You are loved. People
think you are amazing, try and listen to the majority
- not just to that voice that puts you down all the time.
You are worth so much more than that.
So much love,
Jodi x

And here is what some of the children wrote to Kirsty.
(Just to repeat, I didn't read them her letter; I only told
them that she needed cheering up.)

Dear Kirsty,
I know how it feels to have a bad day. Why don't you
just sit down for a little while and start thinking of the
glass as half full instead of half empty? Remember that
it will all get better. This is a letter for you to carry
around just in case you're having a bad day. You are
AMAZING and you have to remember it.
From
Scarlett x

Hi Kirsty,
How are you today? I know you are feeling quite down but everyone has days like yours so put a smile on that face and remember that you're really special.
Lots of love,
Fran

P.S. I am nine years old.

Dear Kirsty,
You are awesome and you are the best. Hope all your wishes come true.
From
Rio

Hi Kirsty
Don't worry about anything and remember to follow your heart. Because you are a very special person to everyone. Just forget about everything and go and do whatever you want.
Love
Poppy, age 9

❤

I can draw on personal experience to reply to a lot of the people who write to me. I've been bereaved, ill, heartbroken, I've lost friends and felt worthless, been depressed.

But sometimes there are letters about things far beyond anything I've experienced. I don't have children, for a start. A fair few people who've lost their babies write to me. I've never experienced anything like that, so there is nothing I can pull from my life but kindness. All I can do is say that they are having a horrible time but that it will get better, it does get better, it will be OK. Time heals.

I can deal with letters I receive more easily now than I could at the start, because I've learned from all the stories I've heard. I can tell people with conviction that they are not alone in their problems; I know because I have written to others with troubles just like theirs. And while other people's grief won't change your own situation, I think it helps simply to know that others have the same problem, because that means someone else has worked out how to solve it, or to live with it, so it can be done.

Hi Jodi,

My name is Claire. I'm just about to turn thirty and I've had a really rough few years. I've recently broke up with an abusive boyfriend after years of mental and physical violence. I've also had an abortion recently, after realising the environment was just no good to bring a child into, and I have suffered multiple miscarriages. All in all, this has left me feeling pretty empty. All my friends have started to settle down and start their own families and now I feel like I'm back at square one.

I'm trying to keep my head above water, but I'm also in a job I'm really not enjoying. I feel like I'm just stuck in limbo, not able to move on because I've got nothing to move on to.

I'm slowly trying to rebuild my life, but I've been worn down and I'm not really sure who I am any more, let alone what I want out of life.

Thanks for reading this.

Claire

X

To Claire,

You are stronger than you know. Your email is full of challenges you have overcome and I personally think you are so brave for being able to step away from that relationship. That takes courage! Carry with you the realisation that you are worth so much more than that. You are precious. I know right now you are feeling alone, but as you start to rebuild your life, that will change. You have so much to look forward to, like rediscovering who you are. Sometimes we are thrown a quick left turn we were not ready or prepared for but that doesn't mean where it's leading isn't going to be the right place. You are heading in the right direction, to a place full of love and a life that you truly deserve because you are now in control. Please do not beat yourself up about your past relationship and the decisions you've made; you have been through such a trauma already. You have fought tooth and nail to get to this point but it is not the end, it is just the end of that chapter. You will find someone deserving of your love and with it the family that you long for. In the right environment, full of love and happiness. You should be proud of yourself and those who love and care about you truly are. You are not stuck in limbo; this is just the unknown and it's scary, but most of all it's exciting. Now is your time and you deserve all the happiness that comes with learning to love yourself and your life again!

You are amazing.

Love Jodi x

There were so many sad things in Claire's letter. She's been through a lot, so no wonder she feels alone. But Claire has shown amazing bravery in coming this far. She is strong, and she should be proud of herself. Time will heal, and I'm sure there is something wonderful for Claire just round the corner.

Hi Jodi,

<u>Letter Request</u>

It's not for me but I would be grateful if you could send a letter to my husband Nathan.

After years of trying for a baby and fertility treatment I fell pregnant last year, only to have a miscarriage in November. My husband has been wonderful, as have our family and close friends, but I'm a bit concerned all the focus was on me, and people forgot it was as much of a loss for my husband. I tell him how fantastic he is but it would be fab if someone else did too.

I think what you're doing is lovely – there's a piece of graffiti not far from my house that I hope the council never finds out about. Someone has stencilled 'You are loved' on one of the storm drains and every time I walk past it I feel better. I suppose this is like that but on a much bigger scale. I hope it works out the way you want and that you don't get completely overwhelmed with requests!

Maya

Xxxxxx

That was a heartbreaking story, and I was impressed that even in the depths of her own grief Maya was thinking about her husband Nathan. People are ace. So I wrote this to Nathan:

Hi Nathan,

This is just a little note to remind you how amazing you are. I find your strength through what must have been absolute hell inspirational. Your strength helped carry both you and Maya through and you are an amazing team.

She thought you might like a letter because sometimes it takes a complete stranger (who you won't think is saying it to be nice or polite) to let you know you are an incredible husband and all-round human being. And you should know that you are so loved and treasured and your wife (and I!) think you're absolutely wonderful. I hope you both have a lovely life.

Love,

Jodi

Xx

I wrote back to Maya later on to ask if I could include her letter in this book. This was her wonderful reply:

To Jodi,

We're both fine – our story actually has a happy ending! About a week after we got your letter I found out I was pregnant again. I'm 29 weeks now and we're expecting our baby girl to put in an appearance later this year.

Take care and thank you for making the world a more lovely place!

Maya, Nathan & bump

xxxx

I was so happy when I heard that Maya and Nathan's story had such a lovely ending. Life goes on!

Chapter nine
We are all extraordinary

To you.

Yeah, you. The one reading this.

The you that's had a rough week. The you that seems to be under constant storm clouds, the you that feels invisible, the you that has lots of friends but always feels alone. The you that needs to stop the world spinning for just one second, so you can catch up. To you who put your heart in unsafe hands, over and over. To you who would still give them one more chance. To the you who has lost faith, to the lost, to those who think they've messed it all up. To you who wishes you didn't wake up, to you who feels they can't see a finishing line, to the broken hearts - all of them. To you who lost the person who would be the one to tell you all of this if they were still here. To you who holds everyone else together, to you that can't quite get over it. To you who feels you never will, to you who's held on for too long, to you who blames yourself, always.

To you, you are incredible. You make this world a little bit more wonderful, so on behalf of the whole wide world I'd like to say thank you. Don't ever lose your sense of wonder. You have so much potential and so many things left to do. Make a list of all the things you want to do, big or small. Do them! You have time. Sometimes we spend so long obsessing over our lack of it we don't realise we are wasting it. There is always enough. You don't have to do something every day that scares you – there is no fun in being terrified – but do one thing every day that makes you happy. It doesn't have to be huge – just do it! Because you look absolutely beautiful when you smile.

You are beautiful, every bit of you. Trust me: there is no-one quite like you on this whole planet. You are precious. Don't think that you have to move mountains every day for it to be worth something; some days you just have to open your eyes. Nobody deserves to be here more than you – you deserve every happiness. Because you are enough.

Love,

Jodi x

For a world so big and busy, it's incredible how lonely one person can feel. So many people are lonely, so many people think they don't deserve to be loved. It really came home to me while reading hundreds of emails from all over the world. Sometimes people feel lonely because they are isolated, cut off from friends and family living far away, but I've felt my loneliest when I've been surrounded by people. I think we've all been there – in a room full of people but never felt so alone. What it took me years to understand was that a lot of the people in the room feel alone too. We are all waiting for somebody, someone to tell us that we are OK. We fit in. We are enough.

Between sixteen and twenty I struggled with feeling lonely. We all did. At that age the solution is to surround yourself with more and more friends, going out more, kissing more boys, making more memories that you look back on later and realise that actually we tried to rewrite the same memories every weekend because they were never quite enough. We all wanted to belong, and didn't understand that nobody belongs, and those who seem to are just winging it.

The loneliness I felt coming out of hospital was different. I didn't belong in the world I knew any more, I felt completely unfamiliar with my surroundings. As if the world I'd just walked back into wasn't mine. But worse, I didn't belong in my own body or my own mind any more. I didn't know who I was. It wasn't just that I had to learn to walk and to write again; I had to rewrite my story, to become someone else.

I had worked really hard on getting my world just right. Each piece was fine-tuned after years of battling with myself. I was finally OK, I'd finally got it right. I was happy. I felt as if someone had come in and shaken my snow globe so vigorously that everything had shifted. Each conversation was like dodging falling debris. 'What happened, lovely?' 'Aw, get better soon!' These conversations hit me like aftershocks. Just when I was least expecting it, something would happen to remind me that things had really changed. I'd worked hard to be independent. I didn't want to be somebody who needed saving, or who needed help from anyone else. But sometimes what we need is to be allowed to be vulnerable, to be able to show our hurts without fear. Being in pain is a lonely place.

We are at our very loneliest in times of crisis, because change is hard and pain is an inward thing a lot of the time. We shut ourselves off. We all instinctively try to protect those around us, even if it means hurting ourselves.

When people write to me it is often because something big has happened to them, and they don't fit in their world any more. That happened to me too, so I know how it feels. A lot of people write to me saying how much easier it is to speak to me than to a friend or family member. This isn't because I'm some sort of all-knowing guru. It's easier because they don't know me. They don't want to see the reactions of the people they know and love, they don't want to feel they are letting their friends down, or being let down by their friends. They want a stranger, a new friend, to see them for who they are now, not to mourn the person they once were. We believe that telling someone we love we are hurting and need help will mess everything up and we will end up hurting them. And that will make us hurt even more.

When I was on the kerb, lying on my bedroom floor thinking about taking an overdose, I thought so much about my mum and how important she is to me. I didn't want to tell her for a while, because I didn't want to hurt her. The last thing I ever want to do is hurt her. But I did tell my mum about having suicidal thoughts later on, after I'd set up the One Million Lovely Letters website. From my mum's point of view, disaster was averted by me starting the project. Although the thought of me being in that dark place isn't a memory she cherishes, what came from that dark place is something she is massively proud of me for.

I know my mum won't be here forever, so I need to find other reasons to stay. Other people who make me want to stay. There are a lot of people out there. What it comes down to is trust. When you've taken a few knocks it can be hard to trust again. It's difficult to believe there are people out there who aren't out to get us. We don't have to meet every new person with a closed heart and our guard up but when you've been hurt that's hard to grasp, let alone believe. The truth is we all need each other. Everybody matters.

It can be hard to trust, and even harder to ask for help.

Because asking for help makes you vulnerable. But the wonderful thing is that people usually want to help. The only thing stopping us asking is a bunch of rules that don't exist. Seriously! The only proper rules are laws. Although, apparently on average each of us breaks 16,250 laws in a lifetime. Don't panic – your neighbour is not a mass murderer, more like a chewing-gum-sticker-to-the-bottom-of-the-table-er or a cigarette-end-dumper or a sachet-of-sauce-from-the-local-café-stealer. But not a mass murderer. Back to the point – what I mean is the rules we make for ourselves. The rule about not speaking to the person next to you on the bus because it's a bit weird, not complimenting a stranger because it will look as if you fancy them, shuffling past a homeless person instead of speaking to them – we travel in singular bubbles.

I'm an avid rule-breaker. I always have been. If I think someone is beautiful, I tell them. If our paths cross and I think it would be appreciated, I'll speak out, because what harm can it do? We are all prepared for strangers to be terrifying, to be weird and not at all like us – when actually the majority of us are very similar. When you break the unspoken rules you connect directly with people, and that's what we all lack. Connection. The nurse who sat with me that night in hospital, who didn't say anything, just let me cry and kissed me on the forehead – she understood that. The rules are that you shouldn't kiss patients but that nurse broke the rules, and her kindness brought me so much comfort. A stranger's kiss told me that I mattered, that my life was worth fighting for.

We're told it's a flaw to wear your heart on your sleeve, but I don't agree. Being honest and kind isn't something anyone needs to fight against. I don't need to 'toughen up' or 'stand up for myself more', as I've been told in the past. When you wear your heart on your sleeve, you put yourself out to receive love but someone can just as easily pour salt into your heart. It's a fine risk to take because when you are honest and people really see you for you, that's when you find true happiness and true friends. Whoever said kindness should be earned is wrong. A kick in the shins is earned – kindness should be a given.

I'm on the young side to be complaining about the modern world, but our bubbles are made a whole lot bigger by mobile phones, iPods, Kindles, books, magazines and the like. With all these distractions we don't actually need to talk to another person. Why would we? We have them all stored together in our little devices. Now, don't get me wrong; I'm not a technophobe. I have been an avid fan of technology since I got my first-ever Dalmatian Tamagotchi, aged six. I just think we should look up from the screens once in a while.

Post is a much nicer way of communicating than most of the ways I've grown up with. I like the handwriting, the effort it takes. It's so much more personal than a text or an email. It appeals to the romantic in me. I liked it when I was a child and we had to phone each other's landlines if we wanted to talk, or if you didn't have your friend's number you had to wait until the next day at school to tell them something. I liked the wait; it added meaning to the conversation. You could think properly about what you wanted to say to someone, take care over the way you said it, rather than blurting things out in a text or online comment that maybe you didn't mean. I've grown up in the age of instant communication and it's a bit much sometimes. It doesn't do anything for us because we all still feel lonely. Everybody says we're all connected by the worldwide web, but we aren't. The Lovely Letters project shows how many people are lonely.

There are all kinds of ways – texting, direct messages, Twitter – to avoid actually communicating with people face to face. Even phone calls are a bit much for some people. So we end up excluding ourselves even more, and feeling even more lonely. There's no reason to visit people when you can talk to them in 140 characters. You don't need to have a proper conversation...

Only you do need to have a proper conversation. Otherwise it's all too easy to end up on the kerb.

❤

My story isn't over yet, and I hope it won't be for decades to come. But while I was writing this book I finally got a diagnosis. It took nearly two years to get there, but it's amazing to know what road I'm on. It's much easier to navigate with the lights on. I have chronic fatigue syndrome, otherwise known as M.E. Chronic fatigue syndrome is a weird condition, but the NHS specialist I saw was convinced. I say weird because there is no test for it so it's hard to get a solid diagnosis and it's usually only considered once lots of other conditions have been ruled out. The symptoms read like a description of my life:

- Mental ('cognitive') difficulties such as poor short-term memory and concentration, reduced attention span, difficulty planning or organising your thoughts, difficulty finding the right words to say, feeling disorientated and dizzy.

- Sleeping difficulties: not feeling refreshed after a night's sleep, or being unable to sleep.

- Muscular pains ('myalgia'), joint pains and head-aches.

- Feeling sick and having palpitations.

Tick, tick, tick.

Although it means I probably won't be able to do a nine-to-five job and may have to spend a lot of time in bed, at least I know why. I can enjoy the good days knowing I'm not allowed to fill them with too much because it will make the bad days even worse. The enceph-alitis I had after the tick bite and then the fits and low immune system brought on what doctors say is moderate to severe chronic fatigue syndrome. The condition isn't likely to get worse – it might even improve – and best of all, the light is on at last.

So I am learning how to live in a different way. Sometimes I still have bad brain days and that is frus-trating, but it is OK. I've learned to take each day as it comes, and if it's a bad day then at the end of it I think 'Today can just go in the bin. In the bin!' And tomorrow is always another day. You just have to do the best you can each day, and accept that some days will be better than others.

Medicine won't help me, though therapy might. I'm having CBT (cognitive behavioural therapy) to help improve my symptoms and to give me some coping strat-egies for day-to-day life with chronic fatigue syndrome. The doctor has given me help sheets with tips on how to manage the condition. Rest periods, pacing myself and changes in diet that may help.

I find it easiest if I don't let myself worry too much about my condition or what will happen in the future. I'm a worrier by nature so this is hard, but if I don't keep a check on my worries they spiral out of control. I tell myself that it's normal and natural for me to feel sad about what has happened to me. I have basically lost a couple of years of my young adult life to ill health and I wouldn't be human if I weren't upset about that. And I don't bottle it up. It helps to give myself permission to feel sad and sorry for myself now and then. I let my emotions out, have a cry, then I can cope again. Accepting that something life-changing has happened to you takes a long time.

Sometimes life-changing things creep up on you, as bulimia did with me. You sense they're coming, but you don't know the shape of them yet, and you don't know how deep they'll go. Other times, everything can change in an instant. Either way, you often don't have a choice about where life takes you; you just have to make the best of it. There are no rewind or pause buttons, so you just have to keep going. For now and the moment, it's all yours – and yes, that is terrifying, but exciting in equal measure. Life is full of obstacles but that doesn't mean you've failed – it means one chapter is over and another is about to start.

There is no point in wondering what might have been if I hadn't gone to Bestival, if I hadn't been bitten by that tick. Would Wil and I have stayed together had I not got ill? Where would I be now, and what might I be doing? Wondering only makes me feel worse. It's better not to look back too much, better not to think about the past, or you can really drag yourself down fretting about what might have been. There's no point thinking that way.

When one door closes another one opens. I really believe that. If I hadn't got ill there are so many amazing things that wouldn't have happened to me. I would never have met some incredible, strong people, like Brenda and Margaret in the hospital. I wouldn't have that fire in my belly that comes with being so close to losing it all. I wouldn't have had the idea to set up One Million Lovely Letters, and I wouldn't have encountered all these amazing strangers from all over the world. So every cloud has a silver lining.

Sometimes we feel as though we have very little control over our own lives, when actually what we don't have control over is the chaos that surrounds us. You have no control over whether the person you accidentally bump into in the supermarket is going to be in a bad mood, but you do have control over whether you are apologetic about it or a knobhead. We are in control of the way we handle things and yes, sometimes doing the right thing doesn't pay off, but I can put the last few pennies I have on the fact that in the long run being a knobhead gets you nowhere.

Everyone will feel down sometimes, and I try not to judge myself on my mood any more. If I'm feeling angry or sad or down, I don't worry about it. I don't beat myself up for feeling down when other people have it so much worse than me. If I'm feeling sad then I just notice the feeling, don't pass judgment on myself, but wait for it to pass. And the feeling always does pass. I don't think you can feel down forever; people aren't built that way. If we accept that and don't continuously beat ourselves up over feeling a bit rubbish then we will weather the storm.

There's a great trick I use a lot these days, and wish I had known when I first got ill. If you're worrying or feeling down, try to remember what you were worried about a year ago, and you'll see how it's changed. There might be some elements that are the same, but mostly you'll realise that the things that were bothering you have moved on. Things do get better. I know that when you are in the middle of a storm cloud it's hard to think outside of it, but the only way out of the storm is to ride through it and things will be a lot clearer on the other side.

If it has been a rubbish day then I say 'Today can go in the bin, I'll sleep it off.' And when I wake up I know that tomorrow will be another day. I can start over every single day if need be. I can screw the day up and start the next afresh. It's down to you. I've learned to spot the signs that I'm getting into a low mood, and act on them: if that means changing my plans and watching a favourite show on TV to cheer me up, then so be it. Tomorrow is another day.

There are some specific, quite practical ways of coping with long-term illness and hopefully beating it. They're just little things, which I am learning to put into practice. It's important to bring yourself out of yourself, even in tiny ways, and this is true for everybody, whether they're ill or not. You need to find something that makes you happy – painting, sewing, origami or baking amazing cakes – and hang onto it, keep doing it. Do one thing you enjoy every day.

I found blogging extremely useful. It's an online diary, a way of telling your story and finding out that others have similar stories too. It's also quite cathartic to document what's happening to you and what's going on because it makes it more real. If you are struggling with your new path it helps you to come to terms with it all. It is also something to refer back to further down the line when there are days when you feel you haven't made any progress at all, as evidence to just how far you have come. It's a really helpful tool.

When you spend a lot of time in the house or in your own company, you have a lot of time to think. This isn't always a great thing as you can think yourself into a bit of a mess. It's not a secret that in times of crisis depression can kick in. You have to allow yourself to be less than perfect. When you're poorly or down you are not going to be able to reach the physical or mental standards you set yourself when you are well. Once you accept that it's OK to not be perfect, it will challenge those negative ways of thinking.

Something else to be avoided is over-generalising – taking one experience and thinking it applies to the rest of your life too. For example, I've found myself saying 'I never have any energy' after days of not being able to do much. It's true for those few days but to say 'I never' puts an added stress on myself that is completely unnecessary. Instead, what I should say is 'I've had a poorly couple of days, tomorrow may be better!'

When good days come, when you have a day free of stress or illness or even a wonderful day, take it for what it is – a great day. If you're having a rough time it's very easy to rule a good day as a one-off. It's a defensive mechanism, I guess. If you don't expect great days, you won't be disappointed when they are rubbish. However, this is not a healthy way to lead your life and will just make you miserable. By diminishing the positive we end up maximising the negative, focusing on things that don't even exist yet.

I have always been one for the tiny pleasures in life, but now even cold water on my face in the morning and the bit of the day when the sun and the moon are in a tug-of-war in the sky make me happy. Love is everywhere if you look for it. I notice the elderly couple holding hands who are wearing outfits that practically match and I wonder whether they did it on purpose or are just accidental hipsters. I notice the way lovers look at each other as if to say 'I think we could take on the world together'.

If you watch small children playing with sand or running water, you'll notice how completely absorbed they are in what they're doing. We could all learn from that. How to live in the moment, through touching or tasting or smelling, exploring the world with our senses. Kids do it instinctively, but we adults seem to forget how to stop worrying about what we're supposed to be doing and just be. We're all so busy thinking about what's next that we forget to enjoy the moment we're in.

You'll have got by now how much I love my pets. My girls are amazing for keeping me focused on the moment, for reminding me of everyday joys. You might have thought that three cats was enough for one household, but we recently acquired a dog too.

Josh the puppy was initially for Mum. My mum used to have three dogs, Tia, Bailey and Missy. Unfortunately, Tia died recently. She was so beautiful, a proper lady, and Mum was heartbroken. A few weeks later, Jake brought home a tiny black and white pup to cheer her up. But Ian had recently broken his ankle and was unsteady on the crutches he'd been given by the hospital. They came to the conclusion that having an excitable, wriggly puppy in the house would have been a little dangerous, although probably very funny for the first hour or so. I was set on getting a pug but they are expensive and I just couldn't afford one at this point in my life so when this little pup tumbled in as a birthday present from my mum, it was love at first sight. I've named him Josh. He's a Staffie/Collie cross, all white with black eyes and ears and a big black splodge at the top of his tail. Josh hasn't quite worked out that the cats aren't dogs yet and tries to play but instead just belly-flops on top of them. The cats are quick to remind him with a swift pat on the nose. The girls are definitely in charge in our household.

It is hard not to notice that within the last year, my house has become fuller and fuller of tiny animals, to the point where I could probably start charging at the door as a petting zoo. Although four is definitely the capacity until I have a house that is a tiny bit bigger (to fit the pug … and a sausage dog). They are responsibilities in furry form, which is what I need. Looking after other living creatures, human or not, is good for the soul. Having them makes me feel a little less isolated. Although they can be absolute nightmares. Letting the kittens outside for the first time I must have sworn about 40 times, had five emergency lemon teas, three panic attacks and one massive 'get a hold of yourself' shake from Mum.

I sound like a crazy cat lady when I say this but whilst I've been ill, having pets has stopped the lonely days being unbearable. On the days I feel super-poorly, they still need to be fussed and looked after; on the poorliest of days they are the reason to at least sit up in bed.

Exercise is often recommended for people with chronic fatigue syndrome. I've never been a major fan of exercise, but I'm on a new regime and it helps a lot. I have had many flirtations with exercise during my 25 short years.

At the age of thirteen, I somehow found myself the best shot putter and javelin thrower at school. Now, there is nothing wrong with being an amazing shot putter or javelin thrower but that was not the sport for me if I was to win the heart of Liam O'Dowd. So I took up running. Not just running, but the 1,800 metres for Sports Day. We went to the corner shop to pick up some Lucozade before the race, I ran as fast as my little legs could carry me and won. Then promptly threw up on the finish line – the Lucozade had been out of date.

My next attempt was Angela Griffin's *Dancemix Fitness* DVD in 2004. Our Ange has always looked like a sweet babe to me, one who by no means looked as though she needed to be on a fitness regime, but if I was to be in anyone's hands, I wanted them to be hers. However, what Angela couldn't teach me was rhythm. These feet were not made to Hip Hop Samba. Since then I've invested in a fitness bike and a rower which have been used to their maximum potential – for drying clothes. So my fitness history doesn't exactly read like a future Olympian's but in recent weeks I have been fitting more 'gentle exercise' into my life.

Now the doctors have put me on the correct tablets it means I have a little more energy so I don't have to stay in bed all day and night. On the days I feel up to it, I can take Josh for a walk around the park or meet a friend for dinner. They aren't huge adventures, but it's enough for me to get out and about without the worry of being far away from home if I get poorly. I'll also do exercises such as skipping; I can skip in the back garden and it doesn't take long before I get a sweat on. Even when I'm having a poorly day I try to sit on the back doorstep or in the garden – just to get outside. Sometimes it's nice to remember that the world is still spinning, even on the worst of days.

If I could go back and give myself some advice at the beginning of the last two years it would be to not push people away. Granted, some people disappear and that is OK because life can get in the way sometimes whether there are extreme circumstances or not. I'm now making an effort to see my friends a lot more. They all know what to do if I get ill and I've let go of the pride that stopped me from letting people see me at my worst. I've started to let people back in. I justified not seeing people by thinking I was protecting them from my illness when actually all I was doing was beating myself up.

You can only beat yourself up for so long before you realise how boring and unproductive it is.

♥

When I set up onemillionlovelyletters.com I had no idea how many people would get in touch wanting a letter from me. I had absolutely no idea that a book publisher would then email asking if I wanted to write a book about it all. So far, the adventure has been amazing. I can't even imagine what might happen in the future, but I think I might need your help.

One Million Lovely Letters is a concept. It's not an organisation or a club you have to be initiated into. To be part of it, you don't need a specific skill or ability. All you need to do is pick up a pen and write something lovely. Write something you would write to your best friend on their worst day. What would you want to hear when things are going wrong? When you want the world to slow down so you can catch up, what are the words that would help you get through? Write it down and pass it on to someone you know – or to someone you don't. Leave it on the bus or for the barista in the coffee shop. Let someone know how amazing they are, because you are special enough to be able to do that. Not everybody needs a letter, but everyone will benefit from one.

It isn't just the person who receives the letter who will benefit; I reckon you'll feel better for writing the letter too. One of the major plus points of One Million Lovely Letters so far is how much I have learnt about myself and that hasn't been through hours of procrastinating about my life and where I'm going wrong or right. It's just happened along the way, whilst I've been doing something that I love. Any way in which you reach out to other people, help make other people's lives a bit brighter, can transform your own for the better.

But writing is my thing, and if it's yours too and you're feeling glum then you could even write a letter to yourself. Say something kind, tell yourself that you're OK, you're doing a good job. Because you *are* doing a good job, even if sometimes you feel like a failure. What would you write to a friend who was going through the same things as you? Write that letter to yourself. Or why not write to someone you know, even if that person isn't alive any more? Often just writing things down can be helpful – it gets any bad or upsetting feelings out of your system and clarifies what's bothering you most.

❧

Life can be truly heartbreaking. Death, illness, lack of money, a shitty tick bite – life knows how to chuck it all at you. But there is nothing more frightening than the power of your own mind. Nobody knows your fears and doubts as well as you and being haunted by them messes you up more than anything else.

My way out? Love other people with everything you have and don't be scared to. It may hurt, but it may also be magical and it's really worth the risk.

Help other people, always. Just because someone doesn't ask, doesn't mean they don't need it. When you see someone walking in a storm without an umbrella, offer yours. Be kind in tiny ways: smile at a passing stranger, help someone with a pushchair up the stairs, ring a friend when you know they're feeling low. It takes very little effort to brighten up someone's day. Even if no-one ever does a kindness for you, being kind yourself will make you feel better.

We are all extraordinary. We are all capable of extraordinary and remarkable things, we can all make a difference. You don't need to be Gandhi or Einstein to be remarkable. Look at the old lady in my street who walks along bent right over, pushing her shopping trolley. It must be painful to walk that way but she always has the biggest smile on her face, always greets you as you pass. It takes her ages to walk up the road but she is enjoying what she has, and that is extraordinary. People do amazing things every day. She is amazing and so are you.

The best thing? I'm still here. I've stepped back from the kerb. My family and the people I love are still here. If you're reading this, then you're still here too. And that is truly something to celebrate.

You're ace!

Big love,

Jodi

Twitter: @jodiannbickley
www.onemillionlovelyletters.com

Afterword
Good things come to those who do good.

So, here we are. The final pages. It doesn't feel like the end, does it? Or maybe it does. Maybe you need a wee and are desperate for me to stop rambling. It's OK, take the book with you – I'll be finished before you sit down. If you had told me two years ago where I would be now I would never have believed you. Would I still want to be here? Knowing full well all the bad things I'd have to put up with alongside the bits of sparkle? Yes, in a heartbeat. OK, maybe not a heartbeat. Two or three heartbeats and a bit of a think. But I would be here, because now is actually pretty wonderful. Yes, it includes more nap times and a pill box but I feel as if I'm at the beginning of something a little bit magical. One Million Lovely Letters has opened my eyes to a whole new world, and who knows where it will take me next? All I know is that I'm ready, glitter in hand and pens in pockets – and anyway, who said anything about stopping at a million?

I've always believed that good things come to those who do good, and to me, the fact that I'm even writing this book is proof of that. When I set up onemillionlovelyletters.com

I wasn't sure whether anybody would see it, let alone want me to write to them. But as I write this, the website has been seen by 100,000 people in 150 countries, and I've written over 1,000 letters to some truly remarkable folk. I feel extremely lucky to be able to write to people not only around the country but around the whole wide world. Nothing brings me more happiness than knowing a letter has got somewhere safe and sound and hearing that someone is doing better as a result.

Not long after I began the project, the people who run TEDx talks in Birmingham got in touch. TED talks are the most amazing, inspirational talks by speakers who have important things to say. Bill Gates, Michelle Obama, Annie Lennox and Stephen Hawking gave some of the original TED talks . . . and now the TEDx people wanted me.

It was the most incredible, not to mention the most terrifying, day of my life. I was amongst speakers who had climbed mountains and made great scientific inventions and mathematical discoveries. For most of the day I felt as if I was in a wind tunnel, with words such as 'algorithm' being thrown about (I had no idea what 'algorithm' meant), making me question whether I belonged there. Before I got on stage I was probably the most scared I have ever been because this talk mattered. It mattered more than anything I had done before, because what One Million Lovely Letters is – is me. It wasn't a theory or a discovery – what I was getting up to talk about was just me and what I do. And yet, the moment I got on the stage to talk, all my worries disappeared, and as I spoke, a confidence I have never experienced before came over me. The source of this confidence is simply how much I believe in my project. Not only has it made other people's days a bit brighter, it has changed my entire life. One letter at a time, I was evidence that kindness can actually make a massive difference to someone's world.

I finished my TEDx talk by reading aloud the letter starting on page 221 to my audience. The reaction to my talk was beyond anything I could have imagined. As I walked off stage I was surrounded by people in tears and was being given hugs by people I didn't even know. I knew what I had written was what I would like to hear in my darkest moment, but here was a room full of people who needed that letter too.

I received a couple of amazing emails afterwards from people who had attended my TEDx talk and it makes me feel both proud and humble to have connected so deeply with strangers. I believe that throughout our lives we will meet many people who change us, help us or even heal us. There are those who will come into our lives when we least expect it and those who have been there all along. However briefly they remain close to us, we will always be able to credit a little bit of ourselves to them. We should thank them by helping others in turn.

I was sent this final letter anonymously from the USA. It arrived on a day when I wasn't feeling very well at all and if my letters bring the amount of happiness to someone that I felt when this came through my letterbox, then I'm doing my job right.

Jodi,

You are the person who kindles the flame for those whose light has gone out. In other worlds and other times they would say you were an angel.

'At times our own light goes out and is rekindled by the spark from another person. Each of us has cause to think with deep gratitude of those who have lighted the flame within us' - Albert Schweitzer (philosopher, 1875–1965).

Love from,

A friend x

Acknowledgements.

this book is dedicated to the amazing people I've met along the way. Those who prove that by being kind to people it can leave an echo, turn someones day around or even change their whole world. This is for my tiny family Ian, Jake + my mum who I hope one day realises how incredible she is. To Kim who has been family since the moment we met and is an absolute inspiration. To Alex and Amy who always have faith in me even when I struggle to find it myself. To Steven and Zia who have become more like big brothers. To Mosa whose love and support is immeasurable. To Twiggy and Sarah, for everything. To Alice for always jumping in the deep end with me. To Katy, Adam and Molly for being amazing friends. To Bridget, Belinda and Alex G who will take over the world. To Anna for teaching me to never colour within the lines, ever! To Ed, for always making time. To Nichol + Toby + Sean for making it seem like london is next door to Brum. To Pip for always making me smile. To Keyla + James, Caroline + Scott and Owen + Cat for being amazing people and excellent teams who make love look just magic. To Liz, Emily, little Liz, Bea, Emilie and the rest of Hodder for absolutely everything and finally to Kate for believing in me and sticking with me through the really poorly days. You are just wonderful. Thank you ever so much. Love Jodi xx

One million lovely letters

Read the latest news and contact Jodi at
www.onemillionlovelyletters.com and at her
own Twitter site: @jodiannbickley

If you would like a letter, email Jodi at
onemillionlovelyletters@gmail.com

Useful Addresses

Sometimes we all need a helping hand – here are some of the amazing teams of people ready to catch you if you ever feel like you're falling down.

Calm (Campaign against living miserably): 0800 585858

http://www.thecalmzone.net/

Calm offer confidential, anonymous and free support, information and signposting to men aged 15-35 anywhere in the UK.

Women's Aid: 0808 2000 247

http://www.womensaid.org.uk/

Women's Aid is the key national charity in England for women and children experiencing physical, sexual or emotional abuse in their home.

Cruse Bereavement Care: 0844 477 9400

http://www.cruse.org.uk/

Cruse Bereavement Care is here to support you after the death of someone close.

B-eat (Beating Eating Disorders): 0845 634 1414

Youth Line: 0845 634 7650

http://www.b-eat.co.uk/

B-eat offer information and help on all aspects of eating disorders, including Anorexia Nervosa, Bulimia Nervosa, binge eating disorder and related eating disorders.

Sane: 0845 767 8000

http://www.sane.org.uk/

Sane offer crisis care and emotional support to anyone affected by a mental health problem including depression.

Mind: 0300 123 3393

http://www.mind.org.uk/

Mind provide an information service for all aspects of mental health, which includes depression and Post Natal Depression. Local branches of MIND can be found online or by calling the helpline.

Headway: 0808 800 2244

http://www.headway.org.uk/

Headway provides support and advice to anyone affected by an acquired brain injury. A network of local groups and branches throughout the UK offer a wide range of services.

Samaritans: 08457 90 90 90

http://www.samaritans.org/

Samaritans are available 24 hours a day to provide confidential emotional support for people who are experiencing feelings of distress, despair or suicidal thoughts.

books to help you live a good life

Join the conversation and tell
us how you live a #goodlife

🐦 @yellowkitebooks
f YellowKiteBooks
P Yellow Kite Books
📷 YellowKiteBooks

An invitation from the publisher

Join us at www.hodder.co.uk, or follow us
on Twitter @hodderbooks to be a part of
our community of people who love the very
best in books and reading.

Whether you want to discover more about a book
or an author, watch trailers and interviews, have the
chance to win early limited editions, or simply browse
our expert readers' selection of the very best books,
we think you'll find what you're looking for.

And if you don't, that's the place to tell us what's missing.

We love what we do, and we'd love you to be a part of it.

www.hodder.co.uk

@hodderbooks

HodderBooks

HodderBooks

To James.
This is a thankyou ★
wonder. The bits of you that you leave
with people once you've left the room,
* with people once you aren't aware of you
you leave with people—
make people love you
about you. You are
Grace who has n
Please kr

Alice Pughly
541 Cobby Street
Gedes

to Alice.
You bring something to this world that
nobody else does, your magic is unique—
just yours and is why you are loved + cared
about by so many people. You make this
world a little brighter. Your smile, your
heart + your beautiful spirit are just so
f the many reasons you are so special.
hankyou - for everything.
of love.

♥ onemillionlovelyletters.com ♥

you make rubbis
days feel alrig